Why Didn't He See the
Beauty in *Me?*

Lisa,

Release and Watch the Overflow!

Thanks for Supporting

Kane

Why Didn't He See the *Beauty* in *Me?*

VERLEANER LANE

Why Didn't He See the Beauty in Me?

Copyright © 2018 by Verleaner R. Lane

All rights reserved.

Publisher:
Verleaner Lane
pourintovsvessel@gmail.com

Publishing consultant:
Professional Woman Publishing, LLC
www.pwnbooks.com

ISBN: 978-0-578-20884-8

Dedication

This book is for all women who were crying on the inside and smiling on the outside. This book is also for women always put others before themselves. The women who looked for others to define who they were. To the women who wondered why he didn't see the beauty in them. This book is for all who believed and trusted that I could open up myself to the world to help someone else.

Acknowledgement

With God I can do all things … that's why I have to thank God first for the many blessings he has bestowed upon my life. I thank God for my girlfriend Crystal Carr who dragged me to go with her to get some detox products and I met a God-fearing lady named Camila. As I put my hand out to introduce myself to her, she immediately started prophesizing to me as she held my hand. We later went to a table in her small Vegan restaurant and she continued her prophesies. When she got finished, she asked me when I was going to write my book. Both Crystal and I were in amazement because I had just shared what God had given to me with her. A few months prior, I was having a conversation with my girlfriend Toccara Steele, and God gave me the title of my book, **"Why Didn't He See the Beauty in Me"**. Her favorite line throughout this entire process has been 'you got this.' One week to the day of the prophesies, Linda Ellis Eastman, CEO of The Professional Woman Network an international consulting organization on Women's issues, offered me a scholarship. Linda has been my coach, mentor and biggest cheerleader throughout this entire process. I'm so grateful that Sharva Hampton-Campbell introduced me to this great woman of God. So, this book was manifested as a result of a team effort with great people pouring into life and wisdom.

    I would like to thank my parents, Theotha Lane and Ruby Jackson, for always allowing me to have a voice. Wow! Who would have known I have this much to say. Thanks to my mother for listening to my Introduction and crying with me as I released all the years of pain but to hear her say, 'You finally got what I have been telling you for years." My sisters Gail, Camille and Mary for believing in me and saying they were so proud of me. My brothers who don't even know I was writing this book. I can't adequately say how much I love you all. My sis/cuz Angela, thanks for all the early morning calls and pickups when I needed them the most. My family is a people of great strength and wisdom. Thanks for always supporting my vision. I love you all with every breath I breathe.

My Divas, Vanessa, Delice, Lolita, Tonja and Dora, who sat at the dining room table in Florida, were so instrumental in pushing me to take this journey alone, but they would walk beside me for wisdom and courage. My gratitude to Yolanda and Laura, who while sipping wine, allowed me to just breathe but you both gave me the breath of life to finish several chapters.

My BFF, Karen Claxton who asked the simple question where did this all come from? She made me dig deeper to the depth from which all of this stems.

To Juavona and Kenny Lewis who always had a prayer when I was exhausted and couldn't give any more of myself. My spiritual mom, Claudett Taylor who said, "Baby girl you got this," which was all I needed to hear to write the vision. To all my friends who were not named but constantly love on me when I couldn't love on myself. You have been a rock in a weary land … thank you!

To all of my brave sisters who took part in writing and reopening up wounds to show the world you now see the beauty in yourself, I truly thank you for your friendship, support and commitment. To my photographer Trina, I can't believe we took this picture in 2015 and it illustrates the true essence of what the title of my book means. Thank you!

I want to acknowledge the support of my Pastor, Dr. A. Edward Davis who only told me to pray and let God lead me. He also told me to stay humble. I thank you and the St. John Family for your prayers!

Contents

Introduction		xi
Chapter 1	Crying on the inside … Smiling on the Outside	1
Chapter 2	I'm Enough … Love Is in the Mirror	11
Chapter 3	Look at Me … I'm Beautiful	21
Chapter 4	You're Better Than That	29
Chapter 5	You Disrespectful … I Chose Me	37
Chapter 6	I Love Me … Take Off the Mask	45
Chapter 7	Live Your Truth … Am I Naïve?	53
Chapter 8	Don't Doubt Your Integrity …	63
Chapter 9	Don't Lose Sight of Who You Are	69
Chapter 10	I Saw the Beauty in Myself	75
Resources		93
About the Author		95

Introduction

Have you ever questioned yourself on why an ex never saw the beauty in you? You possess the qualities of a woman who is loved by your friends and family, you are known to be sweet and kind, a giving person, but he just couldn't see those qualities in you. Mirror, Mirror on the wall, who's the fairest of them all? When you look in the mirror who do you see? What woman is looking back at you? The reflection you see, is she one who is broken, disheartened, unforgiving, has low-self-esteem, needs to be validated by her man, hurt and feeling betrayed? We try to see the best in people, and I guess that's why we keep giving men chance after chance. So yes, some of us have the patience of Job. Our heart tends to see the best in people which overshadows the worst in them. We all go through life lessons on our journey. All too often we get stuck in the situations that brought us there in the first place and we believe we have to stay there. We are fighting for a love that's temporary, so you have to ask yourself if they are worth the fight? We have to believe that these are just teachable moments, and did you get the lesson?

Now some of us get the lesson right away and others, well it might take a few times but eventually you get it. You need to be in a relationship that appreciates your mere existence and reciprocates your emotional connections. What is beauty? How do you define it? Can you look at yourself and see the beauty in you? Do you allow TV, magazines, society to define the beauty in you? Are you at peace at what you see when you look in the mirror? So Queen, tell yourself that you are beautiful, and you are enough. There's an old wise tale that says beauty is in the eye of the beholder. A man should be attracted to your outer beauty, but he should desire what your inner beauty has to offer.

We set out to find the companionship and love from men who are not our fathers. We have a strong desire for a deep and meaningful relationship … however, finding true love isn't that easy. We have to deal with our own insecurities about being rejected. This put us in a place of building up a wall and leaving us fearful of winding up alone. Sometimes we lose ourselves by getting lost in a world of a man, but we have to learn to love ourselves first.

You begin to live in a world of emptiness and are complacent. Most of us don't see it because it is disguised as a form of contentment and we become comfortable in the way things are. There's a turning point in every relationship and we all have a breaking point. The breaking point has been the disrespect of outwardly cheating, verbal and physical abuse, emotional abuse, lies and deceit. You have to empty that hurt, affliction and pain in the bosom of God and be open to love again.

Our strength and determination are realizing our purpose. We have to stop wallowing in our pity. There's an inner beauty about a woman whose confidence comes from those teachable moments … Life lessons. Why didn't He see the beauty in me because I saw the beauty in myself?

CHAPTER 1

Crying on the inside...
Smiling on the Outside

Crying on the inside smiling on the outside. Where does the pain come from? Have I been searching for the love of my father through two failed marriages? In order for me to understand why he didn't see the beauty in me, I had to go on a personal journey to where all this came from. The "He" is about my "Father", failed marriages, choosing the wrong men, positioning myself to meet the wrong men.

Beauty is defined by Merriam-Webster dictionary *as the quality or aggregate of qualities in a person or thing that gives pleasure to the senses or pleasurably exalts the mind or spirit.* In the beginning, I craved for a father who was affectionate and told me how much he loved me but that isn't who my father is. Now don't get me wrong, I know my father loves me, but he wasn't an affectionate man. He isn't one to give hugs or say, "I love you." I yearned for that because it was instilled from my Gran.

Gran was a woman of great faith who loved her family to death. I loved the fact that there was enough to go around for this large family. I was amazed that she kept it all together with a husband who was in and out of the home. How did this make my father feel? Are some of his decisions those he saw through his own father? I wonder, did granddad sit with his seven sons to explain how to be a man? See a man can't take ownership of those things he was never taught. He can only walk in his truth. Dad's truth was seeing his father in the light of not being the best husband and one who put his own self first.

I set out to find the companionship and love from men who were not my father. I had a strong desire for a deep and meaningful relationship ... however, finding love wasn't that easy for me. We define who we are and who we love by a relationship and if that relationship doesn't exist then we feel we have nothing. How could I have two failed marriages before the age of forty? Did I hold on to the tiny fragments of the hurt which bruised my ego? Did I get caught up in trend society places on us? The wife, children and the white picket fence or titles, positions and power.

Are we empowered by life challenges that as women we struggle to compare ourselves to who society say we are? Now I had to deal with my own insecurities about being rejected twice. This put me in a place of building up a wall and not wanting to put myself out there which left me fearful of winding up alone. We compromise our own happiness and settle for second best. What happened to her? How do you get her back? You get her back by loving yourself.

We need to forgive and not allow those things that brought us here to have that much control over us. You need to let go and let God. But I found out its ok to be single and alone ... but remember you're never alone because you have God and you have to love yourself. I look back and say this was a blessing in disguise. Sometimes we lose ourselves by getting lost in a world of a man, but we have to learn to love ourselves first. It hurt real deep and if love is really right then loving yourself is the best hurt we can have. You have to look within your mental, physical and spiritual self on how to love yourself before attempting to love others. *2

Timothy 7:1 says, *"For God hath not given us the spirit of fear; but of power, and of love, and of a sound mind."*

Think of puzzle pieces they are all different and shaped differently, just like each of us. In the beginning, the puzzle has no picture and no beauty to it, but as you start putting the pieces together it forms a beautiful complete picture. As women, we are like that puzzle. In life, you attempt to place the puzzle piece in a place that doesn't fit. Some of us self-correct by seeing that this man doesn't fit in our life. Proverbs 10:7 states, *"Accept correction and you will find life."* Now some of us may use critical thinking skills to mark this change but it may take us awhile to find out that he doesn't belong and he's not a good fit. We have been broken in many different pieces but as we beginning to find our way out of our brokenness and putting the pieces together to find a beautiful you again.

A woman of courage, self-determination and a woman of worth. When you see the beauty of God you see me. We need to live in the moment of being at peace where we are and that it's ok to enjoy the relationship that you are building for yourself. Those things you desire a man to do, realize that you can do almost anything for yourself. You are independent and self-sufficient but as women we want and need life partners too, even if it just someone to have those long night talks with, to talk you off the edge of your job issues, someone to change a bulb, someone to keep the oil changed. At the end of the day, it's just nice to have that 6'2, 210-pound man walk through the door who adores, respects and appreciate you.

Your strength and determination should come from following your dreams and realizing your purpose. There's an inner beauty about a woman whose confidence comes from those teachable moments ... Life lesson's. In 1 Peter 3:3-4 NIV it states *"that your beauty should not come from outward adornment, such as elaborate hairstyles and the wearing gold jewelry or fine clothes. Rather, it should be that of your inner self, the unfading beauty of a gentle and quiet spirit, which is of great worth in God's sight."*

God took me out of my valley from my brokenness. A quiet storm walling in my pit. When did I forget who I was and whose I was? I'm a Kings kid. I began to live in a world of emptiness and complacent. Are you content with doing the same old thing in a relationship? Are you only doing enough to maintain the relationship where it is? Most of us don't see it because it is disguised as a form of contentment and we become comfortable the way things are.

I don't like rejection and I try to treat others the way I would want them to treat me. I have a hard time with someone misusing my kindness for weakness. I live in a world of having the inability to reject others and believe I have to save them. My challenge is falling into a world of void. If you keep doing the same thing, you'll get the same results.

Men are driven by what they see and sometimes it's not the beauty of the women. Sometimes they don't want to cheat and not willing to yield to their temptation. Therefore, they want what they want and that's to conquer. If they can conquer you too early, then the hunt is over. A man instinctively believes that if you were that easy for him to conquer then you will be just that easy for another man to get. Some men look to date women who have low self-esteem, or just got out of bad relationship and he looks to be your savior. You are looked at as weak and he needs to control your situation by looking like the person who has your best interests in mind and you need him to help. My queens, we have to allow the man to hunt us. Remember, you hold the power and if you release it to soon he may stray somewhere else.

So, one of my journeys was in 1985, I met Aidyn. I was a freshman and he was in a fraternity and was well-known on our college campus. We were known as 11 on 11. 11 black girls on the 11th floor of our dormitory. The fraternity brothers would stroll throughout the dorms taking a look at the fresh meat (Freshmen). This irritated me to the core. I was trying to stay focused on my studies. See my mother was a single parent and paying for college was going to be a challenge, so I had to stay on the path to graduate.

Well, Aidyn came by often until he swept me off my feet even though I didn't like him at first. He was arrogant and thought he was all that because he was the campus DJ. Wow, did I let my guard down because that excited me. See I grew up with "Hangout Daddy" (yes, my father) who was known on the Westside and Southside of Chicago as a DJ. Yes, we had something in common. We could identify with the music. Music was our outlet to deal with life's happiness, up's and downs. Music helped to keep my mind calm and de-stress.

Aidyn was the man who brought flowers and romanced me. He always made me feel like I was special and showed it in his actions. So being the big man on campus came with all the ups and downs of any relationship—Girls! Girls! Girls! This was a fight I didn't sign-up for. I started to feeling like I had to be in competition with these women.

See, I was cute and never worked hard to get a boyfriend. Well, I would quickly learn pretty don't get you nowhere. See it's not about the looks. If a man wants to cheat it has nothing to do with your looks. Don't start second-guessing yourself as a woman. There's nothing wrong with who you are. Your beauty lies deep within the depths of your soul. God created you in his image so accept who you are. Yea, I'm short, was too skinny, a nose that I compared to Michael Jackson for years, long thick hair and a crooked smile, but I was who God created. At the end of the day we have to love and respect ourselves. A broken woman who doesn't love herself can't reciprocate that love to others.

It's funny how we define love. Now don't take that lightly because who we love is sometimes complicated. Do you say you love someone because of what they can give you? Well, Aidyn tended to buy my love. Why do I say that? Because when we disagreed or became angry with each other, I was showered with expensive gifts. He bought me Coach and Dooney & Bourke purses etc. to win my heart back. But after while all the gifts didn't matter. I needed a man who loved me for me. A man who could see my inner beauty … my worth.

This was something that I couldn't get from my dad in college. If I needed something and I would call my dad, his favorite saying was, "I'll see what I can do." Well, in my world that meant I wasn't getting it. Nine out of ten times, I didn't. So, because Aidyn was the hottest DJ on campus, he had the money to get me what I wanted, and he gave freely. Now granted, I am a spoiled child but not selfish. I grew up with getting new clothes daily, but that all ended when my parents divorced in the 70's.

I'm a dreamer, so of course daddy's little girl wished that one day mommy and daddy would get back together again. Well, that was a dream as my reality came quickly that daddy had a new wife and a new daughter leaving my two sisters and I to live in a world of weekends, summer vacations and holidays to see our daddy.

I was seen as having it all together but really hiding the tears. People would always say you are a pretty girl but why are you always frowning? What's wrong with you? I was oblivious to how I was looking at the pain from my past as it was following me like a tornado into my future, ready to destroy everybody that was in my path. We put on the façade that everything in great in our life. Are you in bondage to your past?

Do you find yourself as the social butterfly in the group? Yes, I am the person who knows everyone and is in the "know" group of who's who. I keep busy to hide the fear of sharing my brokenness inside. I can remember as a child being so deeply involved in what I was reading I would tune the world out and my mother would literally have to touch my shoulder to get my attention. This was my time of solace to fantasize about how life was supposed to be.

I dreamt of my father and mother back together again, oh how I would pray that God would grant me that wish. I needed my father so desperately to make this right, but it was all a dream. I was living in two worlds, the real world and the spiritual world where I was interpreting what I saw into what I wanted my life to look like as God had promised me. My grandmother would always say, "All you need is faith the size of a mustard seed." I laugh because Gran actually gave me a mustard seed and I still have it today. I was dreaming to avoid all the realities of pain and suffering in a world that was shattered by divorce. Crying on the inside … laughing on the outside.

To be beautiful means to learn to love yourself. You don't have to be accepted by others. You need to learn to accept who God made you to be … a beautiful you. If you can't learn to love yourself, then how can you ever be healthy enough to allow love to conquer you.

The only person who can decide that you are good enough, smart enough, and beautiful enough is you. You have to change your mind set about how you feel about yourself. There needs to be a shift in the atmosphere about how beautiful you feel. You can make those life choices to be happy or not by checking your emotions and what your perspective of the world is.

It may not be easy but taking it one step at a time can allow for the real you to blossom. You don't have to live your life feeling badly about your past. Remember everyone has a past. Take what you have gone through as a learning experience and move forward to your destiny.

> "You fall, you rise, you make mistakes, you live, you learn. You're human, not perfect. You've been hurt but you're alive. Think of what a precious privilege it is to be alive to breathe, to think, to enjoy, and to chase the things you love. Sometimes there is sadness in our journey, but there

is also lots of beauty. We must keep putting one foot in front of the other even when we hurt for we will never know what is waiting for us just around the bend."

–Unknown

So, let's put a pen in this quote and unpack this:

"You fall, you rise, you make mistakes, you live, you learn. We fall down but we can get back up again. We don't have to sit in our mess but brush ourselves off and learn from our mistakes.

What does this statement mean to you?

_____

You're human, not perfect. I am a woman made of the flesh and there's no perfect person on this earth.

What does this statement mean to you?

_____

You've been hurt but you're alive. No matter what life has thrown at you … remember you are still here and you are valuable.

What does this statement mean to you?

_____

Think of what a precious privilege it is to be alive to breathe, to think, to enjoy, and to chase the things you love. God gave you breath in your body to breathe, you still have your mind, life is too short for the dump stuff, so live to love.

What does this statement mean to you?

_____

Sometimes there is sadness on our journey, but there is also lots of beauty. In life, you will go through trials and tribulations but at the end of the day there will be a light at the end of the tunnel.

What does this statement mean to you?

_____

We must keep putting one foot in front of the other even when we hurt for we will never know what is waiting for us just around the bend." As you make one step God will make two, and as you set off on your life journey, look at each tear as an opportunity that you are being washed in your newness.

What does this statement mean to you?

_____

Hopefully this quote has allowed you to live in your truth. Taking the time to break this quote up line by line can have you look at yourself differently; now you may have had to take the time to really think about where you are in your life. If you found it difficult to answer the questions or you just couldn't answer them at all its, it's ok because you are not there yet. Keep pressing, beautiful one.

I'm the type of person who is extremely kind and compassionate, has a heart of gold and enough to give to the world. My mom would always say, "You'll get sick and tired when you get sick and tired," meaning only I'll know when enough is enough. There's a turning point in every relationship and we all have a breaking point. Let me be transparent … my breaking point has been the disrespect of outwardly cheating, verbal and physical abuse, emotional abuse, lies and deceit. You have to empty that hurt, affliction and pain into the bosom of God and be open to love again. So, on your life journey, work a plan and be open to set boundaries and dates. While you are on your journey, enjoy life ... whatever that is for you. Don't be afraid to be open to new opportunities and making choices that are in your plan.

Remember true beauty starts in the heart ... the heart of heart, the soul of loving yourself. Beauty is about your character—humility, love, purpose, faith, compassion, integrity, gratitude and humility.

Why didn't he see the beauty in me because I saw the beauty in myself?

CHAPTER 2

I'm Enough... Love Is in the Mirror

Mirror mirror on the wall who's the fairest of them all? I am! When you look in the mirror who do you see? How many of you remember saying that as a kid? I do … I was the princess and she was a beauty looking back at me. I dreamed that I was Cinderella, the most beautiful girl in the world. When you look in the mirror what woman is looking back at you? The reflection you see, is she one who is broken, disheartened, unforgiving, has low self-esteem, need to be validated by her man, hurt and feel betrayed? Where did she go? Well, she still lives inside but somewhere along this thing called life, she doesn't even like to look in the mirror anymore. She can't define who this person is staring back at her in the mirror.

In our life journey, we have forgotten that our own personal love is enough. We somehow started to seek love in other places. We allowed the men in our lives to tell us how beautiful we were instead of saying girl you look good to yourself. We began to second guess if we were good enough. We needed that boost of confidence from a man when we are well-equipped to say it to ourselves. We focus on the end results while ignoring the signs.

As a little girl in church, I grew up hearing the following story: *A man was sailing in the middle of the ocean and his ship sunk; he was floating in the ocean and prayed to God that He would save him. Another boat came by to assist the man, but he didn't take their help, he insisted God was going to save him. A helicopter came and dropped a rope to pull him from the sea, but again he refused saying he had faith God would save him. The man grew tired and eventually drowned. When he got to heaven he asked God why he didn't save him. He said, "I prayed for God to help and why didn't you help? God replied, "I sent you a boat, but you refused to get on it. I sent you a helicopter and you wouldn't grab hold of the rope.*

When a woman desires love, validation, and confidence, her mind jumps to the end result forgetting that there is a process that needs to happen. We are like the man at sea not taking a moment to see the signs and the things God placed before us, so we put on blinders. A lot of reasons it's so difficult for us to see we have opportunities, is because they come in forms of those things that are unpleasant and unhealthy.

As women, we feed off of compliments to make us feel good about ourselves. Why is that? Does what a man say to us define who and what we are? Why can't we compliment ourselves? We can look in the mirror and say girl you look good, or perhaps you need to put on a smoother or some spanks because that isn't cute. That make up is fly and my eyebrows are on fleet. That lipstick is talking honey. Your hair is on point ... you are doing your thing. Now let's go out here and work it. It's something when you know you feel good and you can walk in a way that you a bad mamma Jama. See one thing I have learned is loving yourself is essential in making yourself feel good. When you look in the mirror that woman, girl you should reflect the mere essence of who God created you to be.

Beloved, you are looking at greatness, strength, determination, a hero in the making. God made everything that is good, and you are his child. When you look in the mirror are you recognizing that you are enough? You were made in the image of God. Genesis 1:27 New American Standard Bible states, "God created man in His own image, in the image of God he created him; male and female He created them." Every string of hair on the crown of your head, those big old pretty eyes, the immaculate lips, your curves ... oh those curves that a man likes. There has to be a transformation of who you see yourself as.

As a woman, we have the uniqueness of being so different but yet have so much of the same qualities as our sisters. Love is in the mirror because the mirror never lies and it holds our deepest darkest secrets, the confessions of the heart. We don't have to worry about someone running game on you because they are telling you only the things they think you want to hear just to get to your pure essence. Sometimes you look at the mirror and you don't like who you see at all ... am I the fairest of them all? You cry past the tears of the woman who appears, but the greater love is looking past the reflection and finding who you are beyond this frame.

You see the pain and hurt of past relationships that started off loving each other. See it's skin deep beyond what's looking back at you. Have you ever gone past a mirror and caught a quick glimpse of your reflection? The reflection that is staring back at you is emanating your true self. The good, the bad, the ugly and the evil. You are looking perfectly fine, but your eyes are telling a different story ... a look of sadness.

You can't hide behind who that person is in the mirror because the mirror shows a person with all of their imperfections, but know that you are enough because we are not perfect ... you are who you are. Your breasts may not be as perky and may be losing altitude, you may have the little tummy sac that you have been saying you need to get rid of for how many years now? Your thighs may not be as tight, and you could stand to do some exercises to tighten and lift your butt. But guess what? You are who God created and you need to find your happy place and thank God you are here and healthy. Your reflection is who you exactly see and is beyond skin deep. You see your past, your body, mind and soul.

So, let me introduce you to Mr. JB who had a nice body and was fine. When I saw him from across the room I was like who is this man? As I walked the room I knew he was looking at me, but I decided to act as though he didn't exist. I held conversation with him in a group setting with my Diva's but looked straight through him as though he was another homeboy. By the end of the night he was asking his boy who I was until we bumped into each other later. When JB and I met, he mesmerized me with his looks and his conversation. He said that I was pretty, and my eyes just took him in. My lips were so seductive that he just wanted to kiss me. We finally kissed, and the connection was instant ... now I was definitely out of my comfort zone, but I just felt I wanted to do something out of the box. Well, that kiss led to us dating because he came with what he wanted out of women and what he could bring to the table. He talked a good game and dressed the part. Yes, finally a man who knew what he wanted without all the games.

Quickly, we hung out and were interested in each other's livelihood. As quickly as the fire burned for this newest, I looked in the mirror with him standing next to me but the reflection staring back at me was jealousy, insecurities, a flawed man.

> *"It hurts the worst when the person that made you feel so special yesterday, makes you feel so unwanted today."
>
> –Unknown

See it went from you're pretty to where is your makeup? I'm thinking like I'm not that woman who wears makeup on a regular basis. I'm a Sunday, going out type of makeup wearer. Then it went to my hair ... like don't cut your hair anymore. I'm like dude when you met me it was cut in a bob. Anyone that knows me know that my hair is my pride and joy so holdup gym shoe you are taking this to a different level. What's up with this controlling spirit? He set out be manipulative, intimidating and dominate. I believe he was convinced to prey on a spirit of manipulation and he didn't have the right intentions for this relationship. His intentions were one of a user, and his only glorification was to get what he wanted out of the relationship.

I'm a strong woman who allowed this man into my life who was trying to break me down each day so the reflection in the mirror was starting to make me second guessing if I was enough. I began to look at "Juicy" (the name I so often called myself) and tears rolled down my face. I began to second guess my own worth. Who was this man that was trying to breakdown my self-esteem? I had to go beyond the physical attraction and realize that this was not a healthy relationship. I realized I was in a toxic relationship, one that I was tip toeing around for fear the conversation was going to blow up really quickly.

Looking back in the mirror, JB was trying to tell me how to wear my hair, how to iron my clothes, who to stop hanging with, I was doing too much for friends and family, I was too sociable ... pump the brakes! I'm a social butterfly. Remember my father was known as Hangout Daddy and so that DNA was pumping through my blood and I couldn't be controlled. I don't understand a man's desire to control a woman but I suspect it's a power trip. That power to conquer and be significant. They paint this beautiful picture when they are doing things for you and choosing the smallest things like meals or your clothes that have you thinking that my man loves me, when in reality he's setting you up to be dominated by his power and control. When I talked, he was intrusive with his words and all the attention had to be centered around him. How insensitive that his interrupting was about him really not wanting to listen to what I had to say. He had opinions about everything and never wanted my thoughts and views to matter.

I read this quote by Wikihow that reminded me of JB:

> *"Controlling people often demean or criticize others as a means of building themselves up and appearing superior and in control. In fact, a controlling person is easy to spot from the constant monologue about how rotten, stupid, evil, ridiculous annoying, etc. everyone else is (Presumably they're never any of these things)."*

Then the name calling came and the put downs in front of people that started to become embarrassing, not knowing if someone too close overheard him. He was pressuring me to take part in his business and I'm no saleswoman so that was out of the question which made him even angrier. His way of punishment for me was not to participate in my social activities. What I had to come to grips with was it was nice having someone on your arm, but I was doing just fine without him, so girlfriend get over it. So, his mere ultimatums of me not doing what he asked came to a quick halt. I decided when I looked in the mirror that I was enough and that I was better any day without him.

All too often he was becoming unpredictable and I was setting him off like a loose cannon. I was walking on eggshells about what I said and I how I said it … things like when I called him and realized he was reading I would say, "I'll let you finish reading and you can call me back later." JB would respond, "Do I need your permission?" … I'm thinking to myself what is wrong with him? Here I'm trying to be considerate of what he was doing before I called him and he was trying to control how I talk to him … geez who is this freak? This was way too much for me to handle. Every day I would say to myself I have to get out of this … I have to leave him alone.

"People push you to your limits and when you finally explode and fight back they think you're the mean one."

–Unknown

One day I exploded and went off ... releasing everything that was in me! See, I got a glimpse of myself as I looked in the mirror and saw the beauty that lived inside of me. My faith had to show me exactly who I was in II Corinthians 5:7 NKJV, "For we walk by faith, not by sight." I had to stop looking at my situation and dig deep knowing that my grandmother taught me about having faith the size of a mustard seed. I was strong enough and wise enough to know I'm worthy of more than what JB was giving and offering me.

This downfall happened so quickly it would make your head spin. The honeymoon stage only lasted 3 months and then his true self came out like a roaring lion seeking who he could destroy. I was a force to be reckoned with and I couldn't allow myself to go down some dark path to be destroyed by a man who was flawed. I had that aha moment when I remembered as a child cleaning out my closet after having a conversation with my mother that I had a voice. I've always spoken my truth even as a child. Most men look at it as me having a smart mouth. So, I had to speak that truth to myself and get myself on a path to block this man out of my life. I had to block his number, block him from social media, most of all block him from my head. I had to take the anger and hurt and not allow it to have control over me. Those things that have that much control over you still have you wailing in your pit.

I failed to recognize that I was responsible for allowing bad behavior to come into my life. This was a hard pill to swallow because somewhere along life's journey I couldn't just point a finger at him but there was another finger pointing back at me and it was my own. I had to decipher and search deeper inside myself to understand where all of this was stemming from ... it was the love of my father. I had to do a self-examination of the person in the mirror. Ladies, this is a process of self-discovery of one's self on how we allow the unwanted attention of a flawed man to be the reflection that is being mirrored. The true nature of my affliction lay deep within the woman that I would discover.

> *"Without Communication, there is no relationship;
> Without Respect, there is no Love;
> Without Trust, there is no reason to continue …!"
>
> –Unknown

So, let's put a pen in this quote and unpack this:

Without Communication, there is no relationship. To have a healthy partnership you have to have good communication.

What does this statement mean to you?

_____

Without Respect, there is no Love. A man who doesn't respect you doesn't love you.

What does this statement mean to you?

_____

Without Trust, there is no reason to continue. If trust is broken there's no reason to continue in a relationship that was never meant to be.

What does this statement mean to you?

_____

Hopefully this quote had you take a look in the mirror and see if you are enough. Taking the time to break up this quote line by line can have you look at yourself as enough. If you found it difficult to answer the questions perhaps we still have work to do.

Perhaps you are still struggling with this concept of loving yourself and that love being enough. So, when you past the mirror you have enough respect for yourself to know that you are enough regardless of what someone else thinks about you. Your partner has to accept your flaws because we all have flaws. Some of us come to the table with more baggage than the other person. It's important to have those hard conversations with each other and be able to listen. This should deepen who you see yourself as in the mirror.

You have been so abused for so long that you can't see the beauty that lies in you. You've been hurt so many times that when you look in the mirror you can't see that this is real. When you look in the mirror you should have that smile on your face knowing that you are your everything. See, men think they know what a woman really wants, but you need a man to build your self-esteem up, encourage your self-worth, respect you as a person, communicate their feelings and trust that they have your best interests at heart. If a woman has all those things from a man, she can walk tall and know that she is enough.

Why didn't he see the beauty in me because I recognized when I looked in the mirror I am enough?

CHAPTER 3

Look at Me... I'm Beautiful

Look at me I am so in love with me ... yes, I'm beautiful. I'm beautiful because my spirit is beautiful, and it runs deep down to my soul. What is beauty? How do you define it? Can you look at yourself and see the beauty in you? Do you allow TV, magazines, society to define the beauty in you? See beauty is more than skin deep and it's what lies beyond what the human eye can see. We need to be around men who will celebrate us. Society identifies beauty by how we look such the features of our eyes, lips, breasts, legs and butt. These physical qualities will fade away but the beauty that lies within you will live forever. True beauty is carried in our heart and soul. I have beautiful characteristics as being humble, kind, confident, loyal, intelligent, loving and a courageous woman. There's an old wise tale that states, beauty is in the eye of the beholder. A man should be attracted to your outer beauty, but he should desire what your inner beauty has to offer.

Take a moment and let's look at being Humble – What has attracted men to me is that I'm willing to put others before myself. I'm a true servant at heart. I serve those in my church, community and job. I can hear my pastor's voice say no matter how God blesses you, always stay humble and learn to celebrate other's accomplishments. Allow your success to speak for you and the hard work that you do will pay off. I want to see the best in everyone. I don't see myself as being above or below anyone because I'm a very secure woman.

I have many natural talents but being humble is about my abilities to listen to others, being grateful for things I have, and asking for help when I need it.

> *"Be Strong but not rude. Be kind but not weak. Be humble, but not timid. Be proud but not arrogant."*

Is there someone in your life you tend to feel is more important than yourself?

_____

Is there an area that you struggle with about being humble?

_____
_____

What opportunities do you have to demonstrate humility?

_____
_____
_____

In 1 Peter 5:5-7 it states, *"Clothe yourselves, all of you, with humility toward one another, for "God opposes the proud but gives grace to the humble." Humble yourselves, therefore, under the mighty hand of god so that at the proper time he may exalt you, casting all your anxieties on him, because he cares for you."*

Take a moment and let's look at Kindness – I'm a woman who has a kind spirit and treats people with respect, empathy and genuineness. People would never know if I didn't care for them because I try very hard to be kind to others no matter what they have done to me ... my philosophy is to kill them with kindness. I love people with the love of God. Some men have taken my kindness as weakness. Having the quality of a human being will get you a long way in life.

> *"Kindness is a gift everyone can afford to give."*
>
> –Unknown

Take a moment and let's look at being Confident – My mother would always say be confident in who you are. Most people would think that I'm arrogant by the way I carry myself or my looks, but when they meet me they find that I walk with great confidence and there's nothing arrogant about me. When you see the good qualities that lie within me, they are always shining bright like a diamond.

Ladies, when you surround yourself with positive people, that positive energy comes back on you. Spirits of transference is real so be very careful who you allow to get into your personal space. You want to be around people who will push you to a level greater than your mind could have every thought of.

> *"Self-Confidence is the most attractive quality*
> *a person can have. How can anyone see how*
> *great you are if you can't see it yourself?"*
>
> –Unknown

When have you felt confident in a relationship? How did that feel?

_____

_____

When have you not felt confident in a relationship? What was the cause of you feeling not confident?

_____
_____

"Beauty may be dangerous, but intelligence is Lethal."

Let's look at being Intelligent – Men love to see a woman who can have an intelligent conversation, as you become more attractive to him. They like women who challenge their mind and just not agree with what they are saying. You should never pretend you don't know something in order to jive with a man. Intelligence is a beautiful quality that is part of your character and you should allow that part of you to shine.

*"Never downplay your intelligence.
Dumb is not cute. Integrity, dignity,
and wisdom are the true indicators of beauty."*

Let's look at being Honest – People gravitate towards real people. With me, what you see is what you get; what comes up is what is going to come out. I'm upfront and direct in speaking my truth. I don't have to change who I am based on who I'm with. If you see me at work, church, on my job or just out kicking it with my friends … I'm the same. I have the patience of Job and live life patiently and know how to wait.

I'm the person people can tell their most intimate secrets to and know they won't come back in their house or that I have an ulterior motive. I live a life of being happy and satisfied.

Lying is not an attractive quality. Being honest is one of the most cherished qualities that shows a person's true beauty.

> *"Honesty is the highest form of intimacy"*
>
> —Unknown

Lastly let's take a moment and look at being Loving – When I walk into a room I demand people's presence and most people love to have me around. I'm an appealing person and most people love to be in my presence. I have an endless love to always give. When you are a giver, it's hard to receive from others. My pastor always stated that love is action; so those expressions of giving a gift, a smile, a hug, a kiss, is a way of showing love. I am a warm-hearted person that is kind to others and especially to myself. There is nothing in reason I wouldn't do to help those who I come in contact with from my job, church, friends and family.

Through my life experiences I had to suppress my love in order to protect my heart from being broken in negative situations. Through life's experiences I have come to accept that some people can stay in your heart for a reason, but not in your life.

A woman who loves is more than just beautiful. She is one who sustains the qualities of her beauty.

> *"It's amazing how one day someone walks into your life and you can't remember how you ever lived without them."*
>
> —Unknown

I can feel Randy's breath on me as I awaken and see his eyes looking at me in awe. I remember the touch of his hand moving my hair back to take in my beauty. He gazed at me always telling me how beautiful I was. His love was like no other … almost an obsession. His touch, his kiss mesmerized me. He made love to my body without ever touching me. What a man, what a man!

He was a man who took the time to tell me how beautiful I was every time he laid his eyes on me. He always said I got you, just trust me. He wasn't a man who had a lot to offer but he gave of himself selflessly. He was patient with me and opted to let whatever I was going through to mend itself.

Randy wanted to spend every waking moment with me. In the beginning, I loved this new experience. He was a homebody and mother's boy, so with those qualities I knew how he treated his mother, he would treat me the same or better. He had limited friends and those who he hung with were few but faithful.

Randy didn't believe in allowing his male friends to get to know me, as that was a no no in his eyes! He said past relationships taught him to keep his girlfriends away from around his so-called friends. He didn't want anyone to get that close to his girl. I thought that was weird that I could only hang out with his married friends or his boys in committed relationships.

Randy was a person who was a mama's boy. I knew that he would treat me well. Is it crazy that I wanted to get the attention from a man because at some point I began to feel suffocated? It seems as though Randy didn't have the zeal to reach a higher goal in his career. He became complacent and was ok where he was in his career.

At the time we were dating, I was working on my master's degree and he didn't support why I was trying to further my education. That started to drive a wedge between us. I was a woman of great faith and knew that my goal in life was not where I was at that point in my life. Something was missing, and I couldn't lose myself in enjoying a man that adored me but couldn't push me beyond my potential in life. I had to listen to the voice of God and move to my next destiny and if that meant being without him I was fine with that because I knew God had something better for me. It was a hard decision to make but one I knew I had to trust God with. Sometimes we have to make tough decisions, even when we think what we have is good.

Have you every love somebody enough that you let them go?

_____

_____

Randy and I were headed down a different path. He didn't have the get up and go that I needed. He was such a laid-back gentleman who was stuck just hanging in the house with his boys watching basketball, football and getting high with the fella's. I came home with one of my friends I was in my master's program with and when we hit the apartment door the smoke hit us in the face. I was so embarrassed and angry that he would be doing this in our apartment. I began to apologize to my friend letting her know that I didn't indulge in drugs and she understood. This annoyed me because that was a part of his life he didn't show until years later. This was a complete turn off for me.

Had I known this from the beginning, I would have never given him a chance. It's something unattractive about a person smoking … now don't get me wrong to each their own, but I chose not to be around folks who smoked marijuana. I may have mentioned in the previous chapter that I'm a hair girl and I can't stand my hair smelling like smoke. Eventually, this relationship came to a head when I decided to listen to the voice of God and bought a house. Just like that … the thrill was gone. He understood why I had to leave him and we remained cordial friends for several years.

Ladies, beauty comes from within and radiates like the sun that is shining on a cloudy day. When you look in the mirror, beauty is not about a pretty face. It's about having those qualities that come from your soul. Having a beautiful mind that shows you're intelligent and have moral values. You trust God should fuel your faith beyond your visible eye.

Granted, Randy and I had a good relationship, but I wanted something in particular in my life that he couldn't give me. It hurt.

It hurt really badly. The pain stings every time I think about him. It hurts because you really care about the person even when they are no longer in your life. You will always have a special place in your heart for them.

Just because I let you go, doesn't mean I wanted to.

Why didn't he see the beauty in me because I finally looked at me ... I'm beautiful?

CHAPTER 4

You're Better Than That

Has a guy ever told you he's not looking for something serious? Maybe he said let's not put a title on this relationship and let's see where this goes. Is he treating you like an option and not a priority?

I'm not looking for something serious translates into I'm not that guy that commits in a serious relationship or I don't want to commit to you. If a guy really likes you, there wouldn't be stipulations to dating him. We understand getting into a relationship is easy but staying together takes work. Just because he wasn't looking for a commitment doesn't mean you won't find someone who thinks you're better than that. You deserve better!

Let's not put a title on this relationship translates to I'm not your boyfriend and you're not my girlfriend just a person I care about but don't want to commit to. You look up a before long the relationship goes nowhere.

Do you feel like you're not good enough? Not good enough to be committed to you, but you desiring to be the only boo? Not good enough to receive the love your heart was willing to give, not good enough to receive the love you desire? You feel this way because you have allowed him to dictate that it's ok to take this relationship one day at a time without a title.

So, what was he really looking for? Why didn't he think *you* were looking for a commitment?

You don't intentionally seek out to love someone who didn't love you back, but unreciprocated love is often the kind that teaches us that we need to take a look at ourselves, because the love he doesn't show you, you have to learn to love yourself.

Are you wondering why? What is the criteria for 'serious?' If you're not something serious, then what are you? A mere moment in his black book or a notch in his belt? Another pretty face he'll remember but the name he'll forget? Have you been defeated?

As a woman, our emotional mind starts to wonder ... when? When *will* he be looking for something serious? Have you ever found yourself waiting and thinking when will someday come? Is today the day? Before we know it weeks, months and years have gone by wondering is this the day we will become *"serious."*

You begin to daydream who? Will it, be me or another woman? Have you ever daydreamed about if it was going to be you?

_____

_____

Be still and listen to the voice of God. It states in, **Psalm 46:10** *He says, "Be still, and know that I am God; I will be exalted among the nations, I will be exalted in the earth."* Your vision will become clear when you look into your heart and see what God has in store for you. You may not understand what's going on in your life right now, but it will come to pass. God allows us to go through our trials and tribulation so that we become dependent on Him.

Sometimes we begin to question our self-worth and confidence level on what we want. Is it that important that you give of who you are than to be his 'something serious?' If you are changing for a man, then you are not being true to who you are. Don't focus on being who he wants you to be, but know that you are better than that.

If we wait on God, that someone special won't have to look for you. You won't have to worry he will find you. He won't come in talking about I'm not looking for something serious or let's not put a title on it. That special one will come with his true desire to be your only one and want to have a committed relationship with you. He wants to date you exclusively and tell you 'where have you been all his life?' You will know love by his actions and he won't be afraid to express his true love to you.

> *"If someone seriously wants to be part of your life, they will seriously make an effort to be in it. No reason. No excuses."*
>
> –Unknown

Ian saw me as I was putting items into my truck. A deep voice came from this luxury vehicle, but I couldn't see him. Finally, his face appeared and I thought … hmm he was kind of handsome. Oh well, I thought to myself … next. So, I got in my car and was preparing to back up out the driveway I heard this knock on my car window, then he was asking me to roll down my window. Hi, my name, is Ian, hi my name is Nina (my nickname they affectionately called me). I remember him asking me if I was married or had a boyfriend and I asked the same question of him. We both answered no! We exchanged numbers and talked later that evening.

We decided that we would go out when I returned from my trip. He picked me up at my cousin's and we went to a familiar lounge to have drinks and talk. We really enjoyed each other's company and found out we had a lot in common and knew the same people. I explained that I knew a lot of people so don't be surprised who I know.

He invited me to his picnic and I decided to go. When I arrived, to his surprise, I knew a lot of his friends even the DJ. He questioned some of his friends about what type of person I was, and they said I was down to earth and a sweet person. I was cool people.

I invited him over and we hung out and had a great time talking and getting to know each other. Weeks went by, we discovered that we were very busy people and we both traveled for our jobs. I thought this is perfect since I was gone for days or a week at a time. I was affectionately called his *"**New Boo.**"*

Ian would show efforts to see me, initiate coming over, he would take me out with my girlfriends, he loved to hold hands and touch me, hug, kiss, and make out with me, he made me feel special, called/texted, and always complimented me as his "pretty face girl."

I asked what we were doing, and he let me know I was his "new boo" but let's not put a title on it, as he believed a relationship should flourish into what it will be. I had heard that line before. Well, he was dark, tall and handsome, so let's see where this going to lead us.

He loved to text, and I hated it because people misconstrue what you are trying to say. We agreed that he had to meet me half way in our communication. We made a point to hang out at least one day on the weekend because of our schedule. He was always on this 'you didn't invite me over' kick. My door was always open so if he wanted to stop by I had no problem with that. He always said his door was open if I wanted to stop by. We would hang out at his place but mostly at my home. Something just always felt off to me at his place. I didn't feel welcome, and he would always say his house had too many people in it.

He had children, so I knew most of his time would center around them and that was cool, because I love a man who takes interest in their children. We hung with my family and friends all the time. I met his sister and parents so that was an important step.

What I found strange was that when I would ask him to go to an event with me he would always ask me who was going to be there. I'm thinking like what's going on here and why does it matter? After he got to know my girls and their husbands/guy friends, he felt more comfortable about going around them and hanging out.

He spent every birthday, holiday, school events and Christmas Eve with me so I didn't think anything of this but something in my gut felt like something was off. This went on for a few years and then I started questioning him about what we were doing. He would always change the subject or fall asleep, so we wouldn't discuss it because he wasn't a confrontational type of guy and he wasn't getting ready to argue with me about anything. If the topic came up via text, he would just ignore that subject and move on to the next topic.

Yes, I allowed myself to get deeper into this relationship. I thought because I had never said, 'I Love You.' I had a grip on my mental emotions and I didn't care because I knew this was not going to amount to anything. Remember, we knew some of the same people and after a few events people started to put the two of us together as a couple. Next thing you know the rumors started and information was being filtered my way.

> *"Don't lose yourself trying to hold on to someone who's not afraid-of losing you."*
>
> —UNKNOWN

We went out of town together, again something was not sitting well with me. I called one of my girlfriends up and told her when I got back home I didn't think I was going to continue to date him. Conformation came later that day and tears began to roll as I read a prayer from my girls via text. I prayed to the Lord to help me have a good time, but I knew what I had to do when I got back home.

When we returned home I attempted to have a serious heartfelt conversation with him, but he kissed me and said call me in the car. That angered me to the point that I went to a picture of the two of us that was previously on social media and started conversation on the feed so that it would repopulate something I never do. This drummed up hundreds of conversations and I waited to see if he was going to take the bite. He did!

This drummed up a place in me where I needed to lay it all on the line even if it meant no more Ian and Nina. Of course, he was like please take that picture down, he's private, and women are questioning him about the picture. He's private, yada!! Seriously, I didn't care what people said and frankly it wasn't their business, most of it was a cute pic. I felt like we didn't owe anyone an explanation as we were two grown people doing what we weredoing taking a picture. I took the picture down because it had done exactly what my gut was saying, and I was done!

> *"I will not try to convince you to love me, to respect me,*
> *to commit to me, I deserve better than that,*
> *I AM BETTER THAN THAT ... GOODBYE."*
>
> –Steve Marabdi

Deep inside I think he knew that what he was doing was wrong, but he had been a bachelor all his life. No matter what, I still believed there is something good deep inside of Ian. He was a nice and compassionate man who was there for me in my hardest moments. But I was his new boo but there were other boos he was out there being with too! I didn't sign up for that and if that was the case why was he concerned about a husband or a boyfriend in the beginning? Ian needed to be honest about what his intentions were and that he wanted to date other women and not be in a committed relationship and stop the let's not put a title on it bull crap. He had to always stay in communication with other women for fear he probably wouldn't have someone to receive that attention from.

So, I wondered why I wasn't good enough and I found out perhaps I was too much for him to handle. Nothing was wrong with me! I have the whole package to offer but some guys just don't want to commit and that's fine if that's where they are.

I thought I was good enough to make him change his mind and I almost did, but that's when he pulled back. Ian just didn't want to do the work to have a relationship with me. One thing I know for sure is if a man wants to spend time with you and be with you ... he will make it happen. If you don't want a relationship just to give me choices on what we are doing ... just be honest.

Are you honest with yourself when a man says he doesn't want anything serious and you still decide to date him?

_____

_____

Are you hearing what he is say when he says I don't want anything serious? Are you evading his answers?

_____

_____

Can you accept the answers when he tells you who he is? Do you believe him?

_____

_____

I'm better than that I saw the Beauty in Me!

CHAPTER 5

You Disrespectful... I Chose Me

Brandon came home and put papers on the refrigerator while I was in the kitchen cooking dinner. I decided to see what kind of papers these were … " Divorce Papers." This hit like a whirl wind … BAM! My gut knew they were coming but not like this! Did I have blinders on? I really loved my husband and was in love with him. Lord, the hurt is real. Life hurts. I can't believe this is happening to me again for the second time.

> "My heart finally said, "Enough is enough."
>
> –Unknown

Brandon and I met through a mutual friend. It was my birthday and I wasn't going to celebrate until one of my girlfriends called and asked what I was doing on this snowy night. "Nothing", I replied. Next thing you know I had a party of four in my house. We had so much fun eating, talking, listening to music, playing cards and acting silly. Before long it was like 2:00 am and we decided to drive to the next state to go and eat breakfast. After eating breakfast Brandon and I were in the back seat; next thing I know

I was rubbing his curly hair. Oh, my goodness, I'm so sorry I don't know you like that, but he put my hand back in his hair and the connection was made. We departed not even exchanging numbers but still wondering about each other. He finally asked our mutual friend for my number, but he wouldn't give it to him. He figured he should have gotten it himself. He finally contacted my girlfriend and she shared my number.

We built a relationship quickly respecting each other's home; never to sleep over but only visit. We dated but he always considered how I wanted to decorate his house because he was renovating his home. We finally decided to get married. We went to a professional diamond buyer and designed our wedding rings and picked out the clearest and best clarity diamond I ever saw. The manager allowed us to examine it with a Loupe under a special light … this was amazing. I thought if a man went through all this trouble to make sure I had a nice sized rock with clarity, he had to really love me.

Brandon and I did everything together. We cooked together, built things in the house together (he was amazed by my carpentry skills), we went to church together, and I rode with him when he had after-hours calls for his job. My life was wonderful! He paid all the bills and my hair and nail allowance came out of the household account. My checking was my own; I just had to purchase the groceries and do the Walmart, Sam's Club and Home Depot runs. I also paid for maid service since he didn't like the way I mopped. Ha! That was finny to me but no problem as I had a solution … maid service, please! Well, that works for me! The honeymoon lasted for a few years and then I lived a nightmare. I was crying on the inside and smiling on the outside!

Brandon didn't know how to express where he was in this marriage; he couldn't come to me and say he was having an extra-marital affair. I worked nights, so he would be out in the streets and not home when I left for work. To my belief, he was still carrying on a relationship with a woman that he dated before me and obviously while we were married. What's interesting is that this woman came to our house and said she was pregnant. I married him anyway.

Can't you see that you deserve better than this? She lied, and this thing got bigger and bigger. Through the midnight tears, this was all a scam because the chick wasn't pregnant but acted as though she was.

I know you are asking yourself why did she do that? LOVE! Have you ever been a relationship and you looked back and thought I can't believe I did something like that?

> *"Emotionally: I'm done.*
> *Mentally: I'm drained.*
> *Spiritually: I'm dead.*
> *Physically: I smile."*
>
> —Unknown

Brandon didn't know how to deal with the woman on the outside and tell me exactly what he wanted out of this marriage. He wanted his cake and wanted to eat it too ... he didn't know how to end the marriage, so he started bad behaviors in hopes that I would leave first. He wanted to opt out but the fear of confrontation that lead him down a path to create a window of opportunity to make me leave wasn't working. One example is when I came home one morning from work all of my shoes were turned the opposite way. I have my boxes faced so I can see the picture on the shoe box. My clothes were rearranged; my clothes were organized by item and color coordinated. My clothes were in disarray! My closet was a mess!

I was mad as 'H' 'E' double hockey sticks. This fool either had this woman in my house or he's playing mental gymnastics with my mind. This was the last straw! I had an outer mental breakdown and all I can remember was heading to his nightstand and I pulled out his gun. I can remember the clicking sound of the Smith and Wesson and opening up the double doors to our master bedroom … I was about to shoot him. I heard the voice of the Lord speak to me that he wasn't worth it.

> "Throughout life people will make you mad, disrespect you, and treat you bad. Let God deal with the things they do, 'cause hate in your heart will consume you too."
>
> –Will Smith

I remember the Sunday message from my pastor and I began to holler down the stairway with tears falling down my face … thanking him for making me a better woman, a stronger woman, telling him he wasn't worthy of me and most of all he wasn't worth all of this pain. He was at the bottom of the stairwell looking up at me in pure amazement saying how sorry he was … the look in my eyes told him I had enough, and he wasn't worth it, and he was so disrespectful. At that moment, I chose me!

> "I really thought you were, HIM. The one. My one. My person. I really thought this was meant to be and you'd choose me. You'd pick me. I really thought we were perfect together, the way we harmonized, the way you made me feel like so much more than I actually am. I really thought you felt the same. I thought you were home. I thought you felt the difference, in yourself, because of how we vibrated at the same frequency. I really thought you were, HIM."
>
> –Payne Hawthorne

I told him the way I came into the marriage debt-free, I expect a car note and my house that I was renting out is the way I would leave out ... but better. I stayed in my house for a year without paying into anything towards the house ... no more grocery store, Walmart, Home Depot, nothing. I set out to renovate my house I was renting and paying all my bills I had inquired while married. I travelled and saw the world on his dime. I was a mad woman with something to prove. You're not going to disrespect me and think you're going to have money to hang out with her!

My world was upside-down, and I was just sick of the manipulation, the lies and cheating. I deserved more for myself and put too much energy into a man who didn't respect the marriage. When I left one year later, I was debt-free with only my house mortgage and plenty of money in the bank. Was I bitter? Yes, only for a moment. I couldn't walk on egg shells about what people would say. One thing for sure, people are going to talk about you regardless. I had to decide to get myself up, brush myself off and get back to my happy place.

As a woman, we have to be strong enough to choose ourselves when the man looks good on the surface but isn't consistent in his actions. You have to be willing to choose yourself to thrive in a relationship. You know yourself and how you would react to certain situations. Do you deserve better? Yes! Give yourself better!

> *"Unless you want to be trodden on, don't be a doormat."*
>
> –BAGGAGE RECLAIM

Be how you desire others to treat you with total respect. You want a man who loves you unconditionally. You deserve a man who is committed to you and the marriage.

Do you see who you were?

_____

_____

Can you see who you really are?
_____
_____

Do you care about yourself?
_____
_____

Why would you accept this behavior from him?
_____
_____

What role did you play in your marriage?
_____
_____

Don't block your blessings by continuing to hold on to hurt, the pain and the guilt. By thinking positive and staying hopeful goes along way for you to stay optimistic to stand tall again. In Hebrew 11:1 NKJV it states, *"Now faith is the substance of things hoped for, the evidence of things not seen."* I'm not superwoman and I hurt like any other woman, so I had to take time to reinvent who I am. Surround yourself with positive people who can support you through the storm. Talk with a counselor to help you make sense of all that has occurred in your marriage. Take responsibility in the part that you played. In Ezra 10:4 NKJV it states, *"Arise, for this matter is your responsibility. We also are with you. Be of good courage and do it."*

Eventually life gets back to its normalcy and you will find your happy place. Have you said things to protect your heart? I hear my friends say they will never get married again. I believe I'm marriage material and whatever God has for me it's for me.

I love the institution of marriage it's just the man I was married to didn't.

Do you carry the burden of society on your shoulders?

_____

_____

What have you done to fix your life?

_____

_____

Divorce is emotionally and physically exhausting; it takes everything you have to offer out of you. The best was to get revenge by not pulling a gun on someone but to do better and look better after the process. There is hope in the process even when it hurts! **Why didn't he see the beauty in me ... I really don't know but I chose me because he was so disrespectful**!

CHAPTER 6

I Love Me...
Take Off the Mask

Most of us wish we could improve certain things about how others perceive us to be. Change is difficult for some of us to handle but learning to love yourself is sometimes the hardest thing to do. No one is ever going to invest the time to learn to love you more than you will. Learn to love the one you are with … You! You have to learn to love who you are even the crooked nose, beanie eyes, big lips, etc.

Are you wearing a mask? Do you need to unveil who you truly are? If you had to define a personal mask, it would be a counterfeit face used to hide the real you. Are you portraying an imitation of what you stand for? Who are you truly representing, the real you or the fake you?

> *"Like icebergs, people normally expose only a small part of themselves, and generally just the part they wish to show."*
>
> –Nikki

Some of us wear the mask for so long we begin to believe that's who we represent. Even as a Christian, we wear masks as are perceived to be one way, but we really don't want people to know who we really are. I always tell people I'm the same person whether you see me on the job, at the club, on the street, or in church. You have to be connected to who you really are before you can connect with others.

Sometimes we put on this false front in front of people because we truly don't want people to see the true you that's beneath the mask. The only person you are fooling is yourself. We find issue in removing our own mask and the only way to stay true to yourself is to remove the mask. You have to do a self-assessment which will allow you to see your truth and show your short comings. This will place you in a position to allow you to make the change. You have to able to look in the mirror and recognize your short coming of not liking what you see being reflected back at you.

> *"Do they love you or the mask you put on every day?"*
>
> —SHIMIKA BOWERS

First, we must take the mask off to see what we really look like. Secondly, people are generally surprised at who they see under the mask. There are some good qualities in you but if you can tap into those qualities that you have, then you can recognize the good qualities of others.

In order to recognize those good qualities, you have to learn to like what you are looking at in the mirror. Just because you can't recognize those qualities in yourself doesn't necessary mean that others won't see those qualities in you. When we learn to love others, so that quality reciprocates into you seeing those same qualities in others.

We have to take care of ourselves because that's another part of self-love. There's a cliché that if you don't take care of yourself, you can't take care of others. So, it's important that you do the things that are important to you like getting your hair done, a manicure and pedicure, a massage, taking a vacation whether it's off to an exotic island, or a stay vacation in a nice hotel where you can regroup from all the pressures of the world.

> *"We understand how dangerous a mask can be.*
> *We all become what we pretend to be."*
>
> –Patrick Rothfuss

What are you trying to disguise by wearing the mask?
_____

Who is really underneath it? Are you hiding who you truly are to protect your soul from being infected and ripped into shreds by what others may judge you as?

In the previous chapter I talked about me being a little girl who smiled and laughed to hide my pain and sorrows I was carrying with me about the love of my father. My tears and heart break displayed for the world to see were only shown as a thin crack from the mask that I wore, spectators were waiting and watching to see my hurts and pains revealed. My choices and actions that were altered were deemed adequate by my friends, family, and the strangers that seemingly entered into my life. As the people got to know me, they were unknowingly lied to, becoming friends with the illusion I had created for them to see. This girl who had it all together!

When we decide to make ourselves vulnerable and decide not to wear the mask and we look in the mirror, only to realize we don't know that person at all. Have you ever worn your mask too long and forgot that you had it on? We will learn that the mask we have worn for so long has become our true face, and the one foundation that has been too fearful to be shown to the world has become our true disguise. That it was obscured for so long by the mask that we have even forgotten the person we once truly were, and we'll be afraid to know who we once were ourselves.

We all wear masks. I guess we just have to be brave enough to remove it one day so that the world can see your true essence. Lastly, there are the emotional masks, the masks we hide behind because of *fear*. For example, if we are unconfident, we might hide behind the mask of name-dropping. If we don't think the world loves us, we can hide behind mask of aggression. We mask the debt we've acquired to pay for lavish lifestyles we can't afford like the cars we drive; we pretend things are fine at work, when our jobs are in jeopardy of being downsized; we pretend things are okay in our marriages when they are in complete chaos.

What masks are you wearing?

One of the most common reasons we wear masks is the fear that the world is going to find us out. If someone came and snatched off your mask will they recognize who you are? Are we afraid that world we live in will show your true self? In Psalms 139:14 NKJV the psalmist wrote, *"I will praise You, for I am fearfully and wonderfully made; Marvelous are Your works, and that my soul knows very well."*

> *"I am what I am. I love me! And I don't mean that egotistically – I love that God has allowed me to take whatever it was that I had and to make something out of it."*
>
> –Stevie Wonder

It's funny when a person you have known since you were a teenager was someone who desired to date you in your adult years. You finally allow them in your space to find out they have been hiding behind a mask.

> "The world is full of precious souls
> wearing masks to hide the pain."
>
> —Alfa

Joshua had admired me for years but finally decided to ask me out and I finally said, yes. I guess I was attracted to him but hid behind that big brother mentality mask for so many, many years! We went out for dinner and all the years of being really close as friends instantly changed to wanting to be a couple! Joshua has always been attentive to my needs. We went out and had a great time all time. Dancing, dinner, drinks, watching football, basketball and softball. We traveled together and genuinely enjoyed each other's company. He acted as though I was his top priority. Always making sure I was fed, and my mother was good. He couldn't fix anything in my home but would pay for what needed to get fixed.

Joshua was hiding a few things behind his mask. First, every time we went out he always carried his laptop. He was a serious gambler; betting thousands of dollars was nothing to him. He bet on NBA, NFL, MLB you name it! This was serious business when it came to gambling. He would pick me up and I would have to drive because he was busy gambling. We drove to another state and he was on the lap top gambling when he realized I had driven the entire trip it, but it was too late. I was pissed! It was an addiction I couldn't get with; he really needed Gambler's Anonymous. We talked about it and of course he admitted that he had a problem. I told him if we wanted to further our relationship I was really afraid that he would gamble our future away, and that I would come home one day and wouldn't have a home due to his gambling addiction. He won quite often but when he lost he would shut down and I wouldn't hear from him for several days.

Secondly, we spent time at my house or always hung out over at a friend's home, or just out enjoying the city. I never got invited to his house but we always wound up at his mother's. I was just lazy because I didn't want to drive into the city. This was strange, and I began to question what this was all about. He finally said he lived with someone, what? Wait a minute, did I hear you right? This is your roommate? He quickly explained with fear in his eyes he was living with a woman, but they weren't getting along, and he was trying to get out of the relationship and sell the house, so they could part ways. **I know you are saying same old line different day.** I'm thinking dude couldn't you have told me that in the beginning, but you wait until I fall in love with you. My head is spinning in a whirl wind! I can't believe this! Thank God there was nothing sexual going on in the relationship. I felt weak and decided to wait this out, but nothing changed after he sold his house. I went out of the country on vacation and when I returned he moved to an apartment but to my surprise she moved in with him. He couldn't explain that move and I finally had enough pride to move on. I chose to love me and finally take the mask off.

> *"The greatest act of courage is to be and own all that you are. Without apology. Without excuses and without any masks to cover the truth of who you truly are."*
>
> –Unknown

I mask my pain with anger. I felt like honesty is the best policy especially with Joshua because we were friend for 30+ years before dipping in that water. There was no reason he needed to lie to me. I was not his wife but have the right to make adult decisions and choices. He was a seasoned liar who started to have problems covering up the first lie he told and not remembering the next lie he told. He was covering the old lies and eventually all the lies caught up with him. I had to remove the negative person from my life because I started to wear the mask of deception.

> *"It often occurs that pride and selfishness are muddled with strength and independence. They are neither equal nor similar; in fact, they are polar opposites. A coward may be so cowardly that he masks his weakness with some false personification of power. He is afraid to love and to be loved because love tends to strip bare all emotional barricades. Without love, strength and independence are prone to losing every bit of their worth; they become nothing more than a fearful, intimidated, empty tent lost somewhere in the desert of self."*
>
> –Criss Jami, Killosophy

There are some practical reasons why we should shed our masks. First ladies, we have to live into our potential. We have to bring all of who we are into our relationships.

Why are you masking your greatest potential?

_____

It's exhausting to live an inauthentic life. You put on a mask or two or three, then take a few off, then put a couple more back on … It's exhausting! **Why Didn't He See the Beauty in Me … because Worst of all, I started forgetting who I really was because I was wearing a mask!**

CHAPTER 7

Live Your Truth… Am I Naïve?

"No matter how you live, someone will be disappointed. So just live your truth and be sure you aren't the one who is disappointed in the end."

–Unknown

What does "live your truth" mean to you? Is it showing genuineness, respect, empathy, honesty, integrity and having moral values? When we finally choose to take the mask off, the answer lies in our own belief values.

Perhaps my attitude on life is different than others. My Grans friends call me an "old soul" which is true because I was brought up partially by my grandmother and I have some familiar old-fashioned values which causes me not to stomach certain behaviors … so with that, my friends call me bossy!

But sometimes this makes things complicated when taking off the mask and learning our truth and somewhere in the middle showing the world our true self. Are we so naïve that we take our truths for granted? Have we created filters on who we truly are and the fictional stories about who is underneath the mask we have worn for so many years?

> *"Let me tell you something. Live your truth right out in the open. No hiding or apologizing for who you are. What do you have to lose—the good opinion of others?*
>
> *Believe me, they have no idea how to do life. And if they are looking at you at all when you're busy living your truth, it is probably with a mixture of curiosity and admiration for the boldness they can't muster."*
>
> –Jacob Nordby

As a society we want to be respected and liked by others. The pressure takes place on trying to be accepted and not feeling naïve. One of the most important things you'll ever do in this life is to distinguish, identify, and define your personal truth.

Are you living *your* truth now?

_____

How?

_____

_____

Will you be the tree trunk or the branch in your life's journey? A tree trunk represents security, safety and good health. In Psalm 1 it gives a good example of a strong, sturdy tree representing a person of God that is on the right track and on the straight and narrow road that leads to eternal life. "He shall be like a tree planted by the rivers of water, that brings forth its fruit in its season, whose leaf also shall not wither; and whatever he does shall prosper" (Psalms 1:3). My favorite tree is the Weeping Willow. It represents how we should let got and gain understanding to our truths. The Weeping Willow can survive in the worst weather and adapt to survive the most challenging conditions but after the storm its able to adapt, survive and some branches bounce back. So, I'm encouraged to know it doesn't matter what it looks like, I have the potential to survive. Just like the Weeping Willow, we adjust to the things that we go through. We must let go and surrender to what life has to offer even if that means some leaves breaking off to see our truth.

This metaphor is about how we can adjust to life situations and surrender to our truths without feeling as though we are naïve. A Weeping Willow based on the Soft Schools states that raindrops that are falling to the ground from the drooping branches of **willow** resemble tears. That is how **weeping willow** got its name. **Willow trees** have elongated leaves that are green on the upper side and whitish on the bottom side. So many of us are like the drooping branches of willow resembling the tears from all of the hurt and pain.

> *"When you are True to yourself,*
> *a whole new Journey begins Be True."*
>
> —Unknown

What are your moral values?

_____
_____
_____

Have you ever felt naïve about a situation?

_____
_____

Does your heart secretly long to speak your truth?

_____

How?

_____
_____

Being true to yourself means your main source of validation is from within your own heart. Based on Psychology Today it states, "**Validation** means to express understanding and acceptance of another person's internal experience, whatever that might be … **Self-validation** is accepting your own internal experience, your thoughts and feelings. **Self-validation** doesn't mean that you believe your thoughts or think your feelings are justified." Sure, outside validation feels good, but it should not be your only source of validation. The more it is, the more you lower your sense of self.

Living in your truth means your relationships with others are about love and respect. It means you aren't dependent on those relationships to feel good about yourself. The reality is that you're not going to appease everyone all the time. It's an illusion to think you are. Being honest and truthful about communicating with others is where there will be a lasting inner peace you will embrace in what truth really means. It can be easy to take what others say and do personally. This can get you in a negative head space where you overcompensate and ultimately aren't being true to yourself. By being true to yourself, you trust in your own capabilities and your choices. You realize that what others go through has nothing to do with you but that is a personal journey they have to deal with themselves. Your value is innately within you. When you are being true to yourself, the externals things in life don't define who you are. My pastor would say, "**When you have internal identity you don't need external validation.**" Living your truth means you have to affirm relationships with others based on mutual respect rather than the disempowering need for external validation.

> *"We do not heal the past by dwelling there; we heal the past by living fully in the present."*
>
> –Marianne Williamson

Myles and I were high school loves and friends for over 38 years. We have shared our teens, twenty's, thirty's, forty's and our fifty's as "boyfriend and girlfriend", then best friends", "lovers' and again "best friends!" We have gone through trials and tribulations. Well, what does best friend mean if you can't trust and speak your truth to that friend? Myles and I have been that leaning post whenever we were not in another relationship … have I been naïve for all of these years? Well, let me set up a few situations that Myles and I went through. Whatever Myles and I were going through, we always found solace of each other.

I was deeply disappointed in how he handled a special occasion dinner. First of all, I didn't care who he was dating, seeing, going out with, whatever you want to call it, to think that he lied so his "oh, she's just my friend" wouldn't be in his presence is beyond me … why would he invite me if this was going to put him in an uncompromised situation … or perhaps he didn't know she was invited too by his daughter. Myles has always stressed that we were best friends so what was he hiding that he felt he had to come up with such an unbelievable story! The spirit told my gut that he was lying but I already knew why … "the misunderstanding". See, I already knew she was invited but that didn't make a difference to me because I'm your best friend. I just wanted to spend this special occasion with him. God exposed him and revealed something to me that wouldn't leave me the same. My Pastor always preached, "Time" will explain itself … if you sit back and just wait on God, in time He will reveal thy true self!

So yes, I was pretty pissed when I walked into the restaurant and saw his little entourage sitting there in deep conversation. So deep he didn't see me, and my girls walked right pass him. He was caught off-guard when they came over to say hello and told him they were there with me. It angered me to know he lied for nothing especially, after he told me that he was just going to grab something to eat with his daughter and his brother was at home. When we arrived at the restaurant I prayed that he wouldn't be there, but God doesn't lead you wrong … Wow! He is simply amazing because he was there! I'm glad I had something else to celebrate that night … my girls' new jobs.

But what took me over the edge was to see him walk out of that restaurant not acknowledging that I even existed. My heart ached so bad that I felt like he basically said, "screw you"! Never in a million years would I have imagined that he would walk out on me. I don't know why Myles was still a man. I still see the picture in my head of him waving good bye to her friends … but not his best friend and that baldhead walked right out the door even though he knew exactly where I was sitting. I felt he didn't respect me, he didn't value our friendship, loyalty and longevity mean nothing … it was simply unbelievable. I guess this is how you treat your so call best friend when you are in a "dark place"! I thought I was the person that always placed a smile on Myles face. Well, tears were flowing … not outwardly but inwardly my heart was broken and how can you mend a broken heart?

I hope he didn't think I was coming to speak to him since I wasn't included in his special occasion … oh yeah, especially since he wasn't going to be there! My alter ego wanted me to go over their slap that smile off his face and tell him a thing or two. Thank God I'm a lady no matter what!

Please don't take this out of context this is simply about why Myles lied and then acted as though I was not in his mere presence

… but I know being in the same room as Myles made him uncomfortable. I do understand that he hated the fact I said nothing … that's driving him crazy because when I say nothing he doesn't know what I'm thinking and what I'm going to do … well Myles, what should one do? I know that I am a child of God I have to forgive him and so with that, I will.

Was I being naïve? I wanted Myles to stop taking my kindness for granted. I do have an insult level and I wouldn't want to amputate him out of my life for some foolishness. I have been supportive of everything he has gone through for years. Myles claimed to be in a Dark Place and he didn't want to take me there! Myles and I had so many missed signals, assumptions and presumptions that we needed to lay down the cards with one another. I really needed to know who am I and what am I really to him?

It is, of course, human nature to want to be liked and respected. But in our efforts to be accepted, we often put tremendous pressure on ourselves to fit in, or at the very least to not stand out in a way that makes us feel naïve. So, we end up masking our most vulnerable feelings, beliefs, and desires in an effort to avoid rejection.

What I do know is life is too short … we can't wait on tomorrow because truly after the death of a classmate, tomorrow might not get here. Our inner circles of friends are not making it to their 50's! We act like we have so much time … but one thing for sure, man doesn't know the day or hour, so enjoy life as though it was your last day.

> *"Take initiative in life by realizing that your decisions (and how they align with life's principles) are the primary determining factors for effectiveness in your life. Take responsibility for your choices and the consequences that follow."*
>
> –Stephen Covey

In this life, I've discovered the more you hold on to which has hurt you, abused you, and disturbed you, the more pain and agony you'll experience. Whenever you try to move ahead in life, you can be sure that something or someone will trigger a response or emotion in you that will remind you of your pain and hurt. You may have tried to put it aside or sweep it under the rug, but the truth of the matter is unless you learn to deal with what has hurt you, and/or is hurting you, healing can never truly begin. It's important for you to know that healing begins on the inside, then it manifests itself on the outside.

Anytime someone tries to address and solve your problems by focusing solely on the outside is providing you with false hopes. In other words, unless someone deals with the root of the problem, deliverance can never take place.

In this spiritual journey, you need to release anything that is preventing you from being all that God has called you to be. Whenever a person refuses something or as we say in the church, "let go and let God," they'll always be a slave to that which has a stronghold on them and over them. Letting go is never easy, but the consequences of holding on to pain, hurt, and disappointment will cause you to be messed up from the floor up. The time to move past negative stuff is now. On a real sense, freedom can begin today, at this very moment—at this very second.

It's important to understand that learning to live your truth isn't about changing or "fixing" who you are, it's about freeing yourself to be the confident, powerful person you were meant to be, and honoring that truth through actions and communication with others as well as yourself.

Rec. Sinclair Grey III, wrote that in the bible we find these powerful and awesome words that minister to the hearts of hurting people when it says, "Humble yourselves under the mighty hand of God, that He may exalt you in due time, casting all your care upon Him, for He cares for you." Please don't miss this. When you release what's in you to the God above you, you must have enough faith and trust in God that God will work everything out. When you release trouble, trials, and tribulations to God, don't go back and get it. You need to know that God has a way of turning any mess into a miracle. That's my word for you. Release your pain and receive your deliverance.

> *"When you discover something that nourishes your soul and brings joy, care enough about yourself to make room for it in your life."*
>
> –Jean Shinoda Bolen

The challenge is that we are rarely consciously aware of our efforts to protect and disguise parts of ourselves that are hidden under our mask, which means that before you can learn to live your truth, you have to muster the courage to dig down and uncover the real you behind your mask.

> *"Live your truth. Most people go through life living a lie—pretending to be someone they are not ... and they are miserable. Live your truth. You only have one life to live. Live it your way. If family or friends do not approve -that is their problem. Do not make it yours.*
>
> *What people think of you is none of your business. To thine own self be true. Being yourself unblocks your energy. It frees you up. It allows you to live from your power. The world is waiting for you. It is time to be you! Live from the GREATNESS within you."*
>
> –Les Brown

Start embracing *what it means to be true to yourself*. When you are anchored in truth you are able to stand firm like the Weeping

Willow tree. You are resilient, so you are not as easily derailed or influenced by external messages that encourage you to minimize attention to your own well-being. **Why didn't he see the beauty in me was I speaking my truth or was I just naive?**

CHAPTER 8

Don't Doubt Your Integrity...

The story of Joseph reminds us that even when our dreams have been thrown in a pit, those dreams can be revived and show us the way to our own path of integrity. On any given day, we can find ourselves in a pit. Most of us find ourselves in a pit that we have been in for way too long. Some of us park in the pit and never move. We become depressed, feel defeated and washed out. Some decide to remain in the pit where they wallow in their pain instead of climbing out to their next destiny. As women, we cannot afford to wallow in the pit but we must put our trust and faith in God to move forward. If you feel like you are living in a pit, just relax. You're not the only person who has been there. The hole you feel you are lying in by yourself, know you don't have to stay in it. Just like Joseph, the pit looked dark and he couldn't see his way out, but it was a direct path for the palace. (Genesis 37:5-36; 39, 20-23; 41:14-44.)

> *"Integrity is doing the right thing.*
> *Even when no one is watching."*
>
> –C.S. Lewis

Integrity" is a very huge and personal term that is always being used. We define Integrity as 'the quality of being honest and having strong moral principles'. "Integrity" is a word that you hear almost every day, but it's not a word that people spend a lot of time thinking about. The root of integrity is about doing the right thing even when it's not acknowledged by others, or convenient for you.

How would you define integrity?
_____

What does integrity mean to you?
_____
_____

> *"With Integrity, you have nothing to fear,
> since you have nothing to hide. With integrity,
> you will do the right thing, so you will have no guilt."*
>
> –Zig Ziglar

Integrity is the qualification of being honest and having strong moral principles, or moral uprightness. It is generally a personal choice to hold oneself to consistent moral and ethical standards. Having **integrity** means you are true to yourself and would do nothing that demeans or dishonors you.

As women, we have to remain true to our spouse or partner. Keeping secrets from each other is a no, no! Whatever is done in the dark will surely come to the light. Someone has to be the bigger person when the relationship is over and not to drag it out but discuss it openly.

We set out to find the companionship and love from men who are not our fathers. We have a strong desire for a deep and meaningful relationship … however finding true love isn't that easy. We have to deal with our own insecurities about being rejected. This puts us in a place of building up a wall and leaving us fearful of winding up alone. Sometimes we lose ourselves by getting lost in a world of a man, but we have to learn to love ourselves.

Living with Aidyn at the end of our relationship was like living in the pit with Dr. Jekyll and Mr. Hyde. My integrity was being challenged on a daily basis. One minute he was this loving husband and then the next he was picking fights. I can remember Aidyn being in control of our finances. I worked nights and one day I didn't go to work and got the mail. It was from our mortgage company and the words were in bold: **Your mortgage is 3 months behind and going into FORECLOSURE ...** Lord, you are testing my integrity as a wife and Christian.

I sat on the stairs and wondered where was all the money going? My check was going into the account and it was missing. The deception of all of this was not adding up. When I approached Aidyn with this dilemma the big bang theory came next that he was losing his job and I was ordered by the Office of Inspector General to come down because he was being investigated for *embezzlement*. Wait am I hearing you correctly? How can this be? We bank together and I'm feeling really defeated right now. Each month the money sent out to the bank, we lived in a nice home, we had nice cars, and the house was fully furnished. This is insane!

Nothing was making any sense. After writing him half the mortgage check I told him he had to figure out the other half and I left for a 5-day trip to New Orleans. When returned I was mad and disappointed that I had put my trust in him. Aidyn was supposed to be the head of our household and protect us from falling into the pit of the world. Lord, why?

Well, after meeting with OIG, they required us to go to counseling to deal with his addiction of gambling. I felt so embarrassed to go before the government and to learn about all of this because his credit card for the job he was used inappropriately. I felt my integrity was being tested on so many levels. That credit card bill went directly to him on his job. Quickly in counseling they recognized the problem was so deep he needed to attend by himself. We agreed to go to marriage counseling but again he acted like Jekyll and Hyde ... oh, I want my marriage to work but I got outside the office and I was everything but a child of God!

All I could think about was why didn't Aidyn consider me when he was making his bad choices? Did he ever think about what this would do to our marriage? If he had a gambling problem, why couldn't confide in the person that he was supposed to value, respect, trust the most? Did he consider that not only did he jeopardize my career but his family? And that what he was doing could leave us broke and homeless? What would our family and friends think after he had been looked at as a man with great integrity? I guess none of that mattered because he forget that he promised me "Forever" and my forever was crumbling before my eyes. My life was shattered before my eyes. Had I become naive about who and what I was married to?

We finally decided to dissolve the marriage because it was not working. Whatever he was going through turned into domestic violence, stalking and wanting his wife back. I couldn't put up with anyone putting their hands on me. My father never whooped me and in my eyes, if the man who birthed me didn't do it, who were you to try?

> *"I can't control your behaviors; nor do I want that burden ...* **but I will not apologize for refusing to be disrespected, to be lied to, or to be mistreated** *I have standards; step up or step out."*
>
> –Steve Maraboli

As a woman you have to stay true to who you are. There will be things in life that will challenge you but don't give in. You have to disassociate yourself from those things that are no longer good for you. Your integrity has to be your number one priority. You never have to question or doubt your integrity if you are living a life that is true to who you are. Life can be really simple if we listen to our heart.

> *"You are in integrity when the life you are living on the outside matches who you are on the inside."*
>
> –Alan Cohen

When was the last time your integrity was questioned?
_____
_____

As partners, sometimes we have to compromise with our mate to have a successful and healthy relationship. It's a give or take situation but you strive to make a good decision for all parties. Have I become so complacent with my relationships that I'm immune to my own self-destructive behaviors? Does my conscious mind really think this is how life is supposed to be? Was this a reflection of who I saw my father as? As a young girl I had to succumb to a life of divorce with my parents. This was a hard pill for me to swallow. Then to live a life with my stepmother and father constantly arguing and fighting. Aidyn always brought up the fact that I came from a broken home. Even though his parents were still together, it was a life of dictatorship where his father came in from work and they catered to him like he was some kind of God. If Aidyn needed something from his father, he would tell his mom and then she would speak to their father. Yes, his father was in the home, but Aidyn had no relationship with him. Regardless that my father was out of the home, I still had a great relationship with.

> *"Perhaps the surest test of an individual's
> integrity is his refusal to do or say anything
> that would damage his self-respect."*
>
> –Thomas S. Monsol

Together, Aidyn and I were a young power couple ready to take the world by storm. We both were college graduates, had good jobs, no children, owned our own home at twenty-something years old. Our friends and family looked up to us because we were respected by so many of them. With all we accomplished, none of this mattered at the end because my integrity was tested, and I really had to think about how naïve I had been.

Don't take trust or your integrity lightly if it something that has to be built upon. It's the most sacred thing you can offer a human being and without it, all of your relationships will suffer. **Why didn't he see the beauty in me because I was a woman of integrity?**

CHAPTER 9

Don't Lose Sight of Who You Are

Sometimes as women, we do whatever it takes to get the attention of a man even if that means changing who we are to get him. Have you looked for acceptance from someone to fill the void of being unwanted? As a woman, it's important for you to show your true self to a man from the beginning. Please don't lose sight of who you are to change and conform into someone that you are not. Are you conforming to who that man is attracted to?

What is it about you that attracts a certain type of man?

_____

_____

PROVERB 3:21-23 New Living Translation (NLT) Solomon states, "My child, don't lose sight of common sense and discernment. Hang on to them, ²²for they will refresh your soul. They are like jewels on a necklace. ²³They keep you safe on your way, and your feet will not stumble."

There was a reason why Solomon told us to hang on to them.

It's easy as women to lose sight of common sense. My mom would always say you can have all the book sense in the world but no common sense, and this is where we go wrong in the choices we make in life. When you stay steadfast by being discerning and having common sense Solomon talks about, they will keep you safe on your way, and your feet will not stumble. As women, it's so easy for us to be enticed and stray away from which what we know is right. Keep asking God to keep you in the forefront of having common sense when it comes to a man.

Sometimes we lose sight of what's really important in life. We get wrapped up in a man and let everything else suffer around us. As we allow our relationship to take over our life, family and other friends fall by the way side. When we get really into man we let it take over our lives, and it's the people we care about the most who pay the price.

"Never lose sight of what means the most to you."

–Unknown

When Brandon and I first got married he was my world and we were each other's everything. I got lost in the big house and all the fanciness that came with it. He was a great provider and I was living in the big life. We did everything together. It was an ideal situation because in my world we were perfect for each other. I thought he had my best interest at hand. He spoiled me to no return and I got swept up in his web to make me his all and all.

Because I was all into Brandon and he knew my story about my previous husband, I finally took the wall down and trusted him. We were best friends and I began to lose sight of who I was because I was wrapped up and tied up in Brandon. I lost perspective of who I was … this outgoing, family-oriented, hanging out with my girls, type of woman who allowed my personal relationships to suffer.

DON'T LOSE SIGHT OF WHO YOU ARE

Many times, we are so caught up in our daily problems and life-drama that we miss what God has for us. We are so deeply wounded that we can't see the forest for the trees. A forest is full of beautiful trees beholden to the human eye, but when one becomes one of many in the forest, we lose sight of the big picture. We are crying on the inside but smiling on the outside. The smile, that frown, pain and deceit is what we are carrying.

There is good in everyone, some of us have to look past the outer core and dive deep into where that goodness lies. So, if you find yourself down, while you are down in your pit ask yourself what was the lesson? Take from the lesson and learn how to get up again.

> *"Circumstances may cause interruptions and delays, but never lose sight of your goal. Prepare yourself in every way you can by increasing your knowledge and adding to your experience so that you can make the most of opportunity when it occurs."*
>
> –Mario Andretti

Always stay focused on your goals ... have a vision no matter what your life circumstances are. When we take our eyes off the prize, this can interrupt and delay where we need to be in life. We will have interruptions and that's part of life, but you don't have to allow those interruptions to be your life. Relationships are very complicated. They can be frustrating and time-consuming, but they can also be beneficial and amazing. A healthy relationship is built on trust, commitment, a mutual understanding, honesty, valuing the other person opinion and showing love.

If something is bothering you do you speak up?

_____

It's better to let it go versus holding it in.

I can remember as a little girl when something was bothering me I would hold it in. It wasn't until someone did something to me and it built up over time, this would send me into an explosion. This was a characteristic I had to work hard to overcome when I began to get in relationships. Again, communication is the key because emotions have been hurt. Communication is the best way to sort out all the emotions and feelings.

Well remember the story of JB in another chapter when I exploded as regressed to when I was a child with all of the name-calling? The disrespect took me to a place I was not proud to be in. For just one second, I feared for my life and I snapped. I remember driving up a ramp and a gospel record was on the radio and I moved my finger to turn the music up to drown out the sound and I began to call on the name of Jesus. I don't recall if a car was in the back of me or the side of me, but I slammed on brakes and told JB to get out of my car and I don't think I was speaking English if you get my drift. He got out and he called me some names that sent me into a rage. All I can remember is my front passenger door was open and he was inside the back-passenger door. I took off smoking with both doors open and never looked back. It's obvious we were beyond communication and the emotions of hurt took over. Brandon didn't value who I was nor respected me.

Are you in a relationship that values your wishes and feelings? _____

How?

_____
_____

Don't give up on each other but learn to talk to and not at each other. That person is worth fighting for but you both have to be willing to fight for the relationship and learn to compromise.

DON'T LOSE SIGHT OF WHO YOU ARE

> *"No matter what happens in life, never lose sight of who you are."*
>
> —Yanni

In life, you have the power to overcome anything. When you look in the mirror, don't get defeated while studying the reflection that looks back at you as a torn individual. You are worthy to find something beautiful in you that God created. You have worth and value in who you are. Learn to be present in who you are. Is there a void you are yearning for? I can hear my pastor saying, **"Just Be!"**

> *"Our deepest fear is not that we are inadequate. Our deepest fear is that we are powerful beyond measure."*
>
> —Marianne Williamson

You don't have to diminish who you are to make a man feel secure about who he is. You are a woman who should always shine bright like a diamond. Your mere presence should be one of confidence that this is who God made you to be.

What is your deepest fear?

_____

_____

We expect a lot from a man so much that we lose who we are in him. Is it hard for you to believe in a man? _____

How did you lose yourself?

_____

_____

You owe no man an apology for wanting to do better. You can't afford to hold yourself back. If you want better in your relationship know that you deserve better. Don't allow anyone to hold you back because of fear, or create doubt that you can't be who they want you to be. Philippians 4:13 NKJV states, I can do all things through Christ who strengthens me. God gave us the strength to overcome times of adversity when we lose sight of who we are. Life will throw you some curves, so you have to be able to grow and heal from what is being thrown at you. You can't afford to give permission to a man who wants and needs you to focus only on him. You have to believe in yourself and trust that God will help you find the "you" again.

What are you willing to do to find you again?

_____
_____

We have to be careful who we give space to in our life. Sometimes that person brings an infection that we have to find a cure for. For so long the man has been spoon-feeding you the wrong prescription. The side effect was losing sight of who you are, not believing in yourself, depression, sadness and abuse. You have to get yourself to the doctor (Jesus) to give you the right prescription. **Why didn't he see the beauty in me? Because I lost sight of who I was!**

CHAPTER 10

I Saw the Beauty in Myself

*H*ave you ever questioned yourself on why an ex never saw the beauty in you? You possess the qualities of a woman who is loved by your friends and family, you are known to be sweet and kind, a giving person but he just couldn't see those qualities in you. Mirror, Mirror on the wall who's the fairest of them all? I had a virtual roundtable discussion with some women who gave their feedback to some questions of dealing with men who didn't see the beauty in them but at some point in their life they saw the beauty in themselves. Let's look at how women are so different but yet so similar. We all have faced some adversaries in our life with a man. Can you relate to their stories?

Me: Have you ever questioned yourself on why an ex never saw the beauty in you?

Yes, with my baby daddy. I remember him telling me one day I would always be there for him no matter what he did. At that moment he was absolutely correct. I believed him but was so angry with myself for being his doormat, I was stuck and truly did not understand until much later. I tried to leave him several times, but I believed every lie he told me, until I decided I wanted better for my child than what I had growing up feeling less than human and the black sheep of the family.

So, I started to date. He found out one night and slapped me so hard I fell to my knees and he left his hand print on my cheek. I had an Epiphany that if I get through this night I'm disappearing and running for my life. That one and only time he hit me, he also slapped every bit of feelings I had for me. I left and never looked back. I began to believe that I was all I had and if I don't protect, love and value myself no one else will.. I did some promiscuous things that I had to do, not proud of myself, but I had to find myself. I shut down, turned people out and built a wall around my heart to protect myself. It made me a no-nonsense person, some called me mean and selfish, but I considered it protecting me. This attracted different type of men that where interested in me. Men like a chase and not one who is needy and always available aka (act thirsty).

Me: Why didn't he see the beauty in you?

"Because I truly didn't feel worthy or beautiful, instead I felt desperate, insecure and ugly for a long time until I met someone who put me first. He saw something I didn't see in myself and he loved me for all of my faults/demons. He also put my son first and I never asked him, but he just knew that was a priority. It was the first time I had unconditional love from a man who didn't want anything but me and my son.
I am still waiting on him to wake up one day and say I'm leaving. God sent him to me just when I was not looking. He found me a man who finds a wife a good thing. If a man is interested, he will move heaven and earth to be with you ... if you are the one. If not, you're wasting your precious time and energy. Your Boaz will not find you because you are with someone God has not sent. You will know it when he calls just

to say I was thinking about you, or how are you feeling, I miss you. He knows what you need before you do. Love doesn't hurt. Instead, he should make you feel like the queen you are ..."

–LADY DAY

I can relate to Lady Day when after leaving Aidyn I went to live with my sister. Aidyn stalked me at home, at work. One day he asked if we could talk and my sister and brother-in-law were sitting on the front porch and I got in the parked car with Aidyn. He said he wanted his wife back. I said no, and he punched me dead in the face. I fought for my life in that car so much that my sister noticed the car was rocking back and forth and they came to my rescue. The police were called, and I had to file an order of protection which went on his record and kept him from getting some jobs he wanted. I explained in another chapter that my daddy never whooped me, so I couldn't see myself getting beaten by a man. I too left and never turned back.

When I look in the mirror I see one of God's greatest creation. A Woman, strong, intelligent and beautiful from the inside out. I am reminded of a quote by the late Miles Monroe, God's love sets us free from the need to seek approval. Knowing that we are loved by God, accepted by God, approved by God, and that we are new creations in Christ, empowers us to reject self-rejection and embrace a healthy self-love. Being secure in God's love for us, our love for Him, and our love for ourselves.

When the purpose of a thing is unknown, abuse is inevitable. So, when I open myself up to a relationship I put all my cards on the table in the beginning, no time for games.

I put my cards on the table too with Brandon and low and behold didn't he shatter my heart by using the very thing that I had shared to hurt me all over?

Me: Why he didn't see my beauty?

"Because he's not ready for the kind of woman I am. Most men aren't wired to notice obvious signs that a

particular love interest is the right match for him until it's no longer in front of him. That's when he becomes aware of who you really are and open to life that you have created for yourself then he's all in with you, or out because he's not strong enough to let you shine."

–Buss

Me: Have you ever questioned yourself on why an ex never saw the beauty in you?

I believe my ex's have always seen the beauty in me. All of them treated me like a beautiful princess. Even the abusive bipolar 2nd husband who bought me lavish gifts and loved showing me off but thankfully I quickly got away from that psycho. When I look in the mirror I see a beautiful woman that can have any man she wants which is probably why I'm the one who leaves the relationship. My issue is stability. And I'm learning that with Craig. He's perfect for me. He stops me from running away when things get difficult.

Me: Even though the Bi-Polar husband showered you with gifts as it relates to your relationship, what it about you that he felt like abuse had to happen? This affected you so much that you had a culture of running from relationships.

"I was running long before husband #2. I never loved him. I was just using him to run from my first husband. I met him during my first divorce and he took care of me and the girls. I had no intention of marrying him, but he said I had to or he would leave me, and I was a fugitive on the run, so I couldn't go home or work. This is why I put up with the abuse. The abuse did not cause the damage I was used to by being abused as a child from my grandmother. It did teach me the Karma of using people, and how powerful I truly was.

In the midst of my last abusive episode, I shouted silently in my head "No More!" And he suddenly stopped and walked away. He never touched me again. In fact, no one has ever laid a hand on me since that moment. Thanks for making me think about why I run. And not just from relationships but from jobs, goals and life in general. I know it stems from my childhood and I've got a lot of inner work still to do."

–Elisabeth Tayler

Elisabeth Tayler – early on I would do the same thing. My philosophy in life was I going to do you before you do me, so I would run away from relationships too.

Me: Have you ever questioned yourself on why an ex never saw the beauty in you?

Yes, I think because I am such an independent and direct woman, I have been told that I can be intimidating, and a man feels like there would be nothing he could do for me.

Angel Eyes – *it's funny that you say that because I heard similar things stated to me like I'm unapproachable.*

Me: When you look in the mirror who do you see?

I see a woman who is strong in the Lord but who also is guarded due to past hurts and desires the love that she gives others.

Why didn't he see the beauty in you?

"He couldn't see past the fact that even though I come off strong, direct and independent, I am still a woman that desires to be loved and taken care of by her man."

–Angel Eyes

Have you ever questioned yourself on why an ex never saw the beauty in you?

I think every woman that experienced a failed relationship has always gone to the mirror and questioned what happened ... what did I do wrong? This statement is especially true if we were blind-sided and didn't see a breakup coming or maybe not even a break up but someone else has entered the picture with you and your guy. Both of these scenarios are painful and has resulted in me standing in front of a mirror to figure out what went wrong.

KC – this is oh too familiar. I felt the same way when Myles decided that he was in a dark place. I was thinking every time I give you another chance and we get to that certain place the break up occurs and he is using silly reasons like it's your job, you're never in town, but I was busting my butt to get home for the weekend, and he magically decides to take on another job ... Really Myles!

When you look in the mirror who do you see?

The beauty he once saw in me, I felt was no more. So why look in the mirror? Was it only a physical appearance they were interested in or was it much more than the physical? Yes, it was more than the physical appearance, it was my entire make-up that initially won his love. I am a successful, independent, strong black woman who exudes kindness, greets you with a dazzling smile, will shower you with unconditional love, keeps things 100% honest, enjoys giving, and has high family standards. These are a few characteristics that I offered in my relationships and learned that this was not always sufficient. So, I'll ask why didn't any of them see the jewel they had?

Why didn't he see the beauty in you?

> "After enough breakups, I finally understood that I can't and shouldn't question my beauty because I know it is found deep down in my soul and shines bright on the outside. I'm not afraid to go to the mirror and look at myself for

errors, but I also look to make sure that I remain scratch free. Sometimes the ones we date and maybe at some point even may love, don't always see us through the same lens."

–KC

When you look in the mirror who do you see?

*When I look in the mirror I see a woman that is confident, poised but sometimes I question myself, I start with a yes then I second guess myself and end with a no. Sometimes I put on a red lipstick, when I know I'm a neutral **barely there** gal. (That's how I perceived myself thru my mirror at 10x magnification).*

Why didn't he see the beauty in you?

*Thus, my previous relationships were driven by how I acted unsure, second guessing myself, and under-estimating my true worth. I realized in order for my person to see the beauty in me, I had to make confident decisions and set requirements for my future relationships (No more settling for **Barely There** situations). With that all said, no one would see the Beauty in me until I started to display my beautiful qualities!*

As of today, I'm confident, I'm on the right path!

–#WEDDINGBELLE

Weddingbelle – when I decided to make a confident decision to choose me over him, I started to see my beautiful qualities. That's why I can go to restaurant alone, grab a movie by myself, etc. because I'm confident in who I am.

I thought if I tried to be everything he wanted, that would be enough. Enough to make him happy. Enough for him to want me for me. I wondered about this time and time again. After failed relationships, I had to take a look at me and ask myself, What's wrong with me? What was

I doing or not doing? I looked at the woman in the mirror. I saw a girl that was trying to look like a woman. Strong I wasn't, confident I wasn't. Was he picking up on these things? I was looking for someone to love me. Did I love myself? I had insecurities. I doubted myself and what I was capable of. I allowed him to break my self-esteem. I became vulnerable.

So how could he see the beauty in me if I couldn't see it myself? In his eyes, I was probably weak and easy. I gave myself so easily, thinking sex was love. I acted like I had it going on, which was far from the truth. Like the saying goes ... you can be beautiful on the outside, but ugly on the inside. So, I had to start loving me, encouraging myself. Getting myself in order, dealing with my pain. So now, my beauty within will show outward.

> "Don't get me wrong, I'm not perfect. I'm still a work in progress. I am becoming a better me. I still have challenges, but it's how I handle them now. With God I can, and I will."
>
> –Specialk

Specialk – wow! this sounds like my relationship with Ian trying to be his everything and everybody he wanted me to be. I was vulnerable to who and what he wanted me to be and not confident to say who I was.

When you look in the mirror who do you see?

When I look in the mirror I see a girl who always felt like she was the total package for any man. Smart, funny, cute, talented, and sweet. I see a girl who loves hard and will sacrifice anything for those she cares about.

Baby Girl – *I love hard too and some deserved my love and others didn't.*

Why didn't he see the beauty in you?

> "He didn't see the beauty in me because he was blinded by lust and false expectations of what a real woman is and what

a real woman offers. He didn't see the beauty because I was so busy trying to please him, that I neglected to care for myself."

–Baby Girl

This is my spin on the question.

"Why Didn't He See the Beauty in Me',

The question at hand is the end result of what we internally give outward; you have to find and have self-love and beauty before you can receive it from another. It's unrealistic to expect someone to find your beauty if you yourself have not discovered such. Queens have to know who they are and where their beauty flows from because if they do not know, neither will their partners. Knowing your Beauty, Worth and Self Love comes from your inner glow which is the God within You, and if you have not discovered it, no one else will.

> "He will not see your inner scope if you do not .Women have the obligation of Self Preservation. It starts from the very first look in the mirror by getting affirmations and being taught about self-worth from an early start as a little queen. It's about having a strong sense of self-worth. Women who have strength and inner beauty know their worth and will partner with another who celebrates her inner zeal. Those who did not receive self-worth affirmations while young will actually need to acquire such to break the cycle of low self-worth and esteem, because what you feel is what you attract."

–KenndiTaylor

KenndiTaylor – it took me years to know my beauty that lies within me. Now I know I'm worthy and I have self-love for myself.

"In answering the author's question, one would really have to care what the man thought. I myself have gone through a journey that puts minimum value on external forces. What's more important is how I feel about myself. And I have found that the more confident that I am in myself and the more authentic I am to myself, the more people of quality I attract. When I say 'of quality', these are the ones who possess the characteristics that I feel necessary to propel me further or to induce or help me in my growth on my life's Journey. Now don't get me wrong, I wasn't born like that. It came with trials and tribulations, hurt, heartache, pain, and self-exploration. I think the key to a woman's journey is love thyself first and honestly don't give a flying care what anybody else thinks. When I look at the mirror on the wall, I see a beautiful soul, a God loving person, a person with full potential. It doesn't matter the size and shape of my eyes, my nose, my mouth, or my butt ... and it's huge! Who I see is irrelevant to who I am, but because of who I am, who you see is me."

–Intimate Whisperer

Intimate Whisperer – I thank God for being a God-fearing woman who knows I'm full of potential because of all my accomplishments.

Me: Why didn't he see the beauty in me?

Could it be that I didn't believe in the beauty I saw in myself from time to time and acted in ways which compromised who I am as woman? As a woman, there are times when we desire for the "right" man to see all we possess as powerful women. Could it be that "he" was not supposed to see our full beauty from the inside and out due to us not being ready for all of our beauty to be revealed? Or better yet, him being able to handle all of this **SHE POWER** *we bring to any relationship?*

I SAW THE BEAUTY IN MYSELF

> "This question is one which many women toss back and forth in their brains. I know I do from time to time when I like a man and he acts like I am not enough. One thing I had to realize was the value I have in **SELF**. I love me and there is no way I am going to allow anyone to treat me less than, when I know I was created to be **GREATER THAN**. I can say with the help of trials and tests, when I look at myself in the mirror, I see beauty, love, kindness, and a powerful woman."
>
> –NicoleShePower S.

NicoleShePower S – as I ponder over what you have shared, most of the men who have been in my life can't handle the ShePower that I have been blessed with. Instead of embracing what I brought to the table, they tried to make me feel I was not worthy.

Why Didn't He See the Beauty in Me"?

The Beauty in me was not seen with the eyes, it was to be felt with the heart and soul! The beauty in me was young and in full blossom! It could have been grown and cultivated by him into a beautiful flower garden – a strong woman allowed to shine or cultivated into a strong forest – a strong woman with a lot to offer him and the world. Both are beautiful creations of God!

> "In the beginning, there was wining, dining and fun, the landscape was being cultivated for a beautiful flower garden, but then life and reality happened. Instead of pruning the garden, he left the upkeep to me. Instead of beautiful flowers, strong trees began to take over the garden. He was threatened by the overtaking of the trees and often tried to cut the trees down, but my roots run deep and strong! He was not wise enough to appreciate the year-round food, shelter and comfort

that my beautiful forest provided us; he only stayed focused on the seasonal beauty that the beautiful flower garden supplied. It is his loss that he "couldn't see the forest for the trees".

–Sandy

Sandy – it's sad when a man wines and dines you and then when he feels he got you where he wants you, we are left out in the wilderness to fend for ourselves.

Have I ever questioned myself on why an ex never saw the beauty in me?

Well my young adult self, when I was in my 20's has. My ex would agree that I was a nice looking young lady, possessed great qualities, and came from a decent family. In fact, he would even say that I was marriage material and that he had even proposed several times. However, because he cheated and lied before and after our child was born AND before and after the proposal, I became more and more upset as well. How could he do this to me? I treated him well, was nice to him and respected our relationship. I often had the 2 personalities on my shoulders trying to figure out what should I do. The pissed off and upset personality would tell me, "you don't need him, there are other men out here who would love to have a relationship with you and respect you."

On the flip side, the confused personality would say things like, "he does love you, that's why he proposed, that's why he keeps coming back. Maybe if you dress sexier.". Aww, but the truth of the matter was that I eventually came to realize (after the 3rd cheating incident or at least the 3rd one that I was aware of) was that although I was questioning **why he didn't see the beauty in me** *and trying to come up with ways I could improve my relationship and myself so that he could see my beauty, he did see the beauty in me. He was just greedy. He wanted his cake and wanted to eat it too.*

"My adult self is much more mature and wiser. I know who I am and for the most part I like who I am. Yeah, I can afford to lose some pounds, but when it comes to a relationship with a man, I no longer give a man the opportunity to treat me less than the queen that I am. However, as I say this, I have to also admit that every now and then I wonder if there is something wrong with me. I wonder this at times because I recognize that a man has not tried to come on to me and that makes me wonder if I'm attractive. Every woman enjoys a little attention every now and then. However, as soon as the thought enters my mind, I quickly dismiss it and tell myself that I'm a beautiful woman."

–Dominique Deveron

So many times, I have questioned myself too, Dominique Deveron, asking is something wrong with me? I can remember having a conversation with Myles and him telling me nothing is wrong with me, but I need to let a man be a man. My personality is so dominant around getting things done that I don't need a man to do that! I have cheated myself out of so much.

Why Didn't He See the Beauty in Me"?

I've questioned myself countless times as to **why he never saw the beauty in me**. It wasn't that he didn't see the beauty in me it was that he didn't see the beauty in himself; therefore he wasn't able to see me for who I really was. When a person is depressed and has low self-esteem it's hard to give what you don't have in you. It wasn't hard for him to see the qualities in me; it was hard for him to accept the love that was given and shown to me by family and friends.

When you look in the mirror who do you see?

> *"When I look in the mirror I see a very strong, compassionate and caring woman. I see a woman that loves very hard and takes her time to decide on relationships. I see a woman who has been hurt before but still manages to let the wall down just enough to let the new in. A woman that with God's help and guidance will try again."*
>
> –SHENE

Shene – when I read your story this brought me back to JB. How could he see what I had to offer when he was dealing with his own demons, depression and self-esteem issues?

I think the men I was involved with didn't really see me because I didn't allow myself to be truly and authentically seen. Oh, I allowed them SOME access, just not total access. If I were to be completely honest, I'd have to admit that I've sabotaged a relationship or two, or even three (lol), in my time.

I could blame it on being hurt, or even rejected in the past; but the truth of the matter is that I simply didn't want to risk true intimacy and all the accoutrements that come with it!

Back then, I felt like if I allowed myself to give in and risk true intimacy, it would get in the way of everything else I was socialized and raised to do and accomplish in my life.

All my life I've been the responsible one. The one who made sure everyone had everything and everyone they needed, often to the detriment of myself. I come from a family of givers and I was raised in the church, so putting myself ahead of others was never a well-received option in my world.

It wasn't until I was in college and met a man who lived to please me that I learned and saw first-hand how the other half lived. He genuinely liked me as a person and loved me as a woman. He treated me with tenderness and affection, showed me that I am more than enough, and that I deserve to be loved. He also taught me what it is to be a well-loved woman in every way; that my emotions as well as my body needed attention and nurturing. I didn't make things easy for him AT ALL, because I knew if I stopped fighting it, I was going to fall deeply in love with him (and boy did I).

> "I was never the same after that love affair! Because I could no longer accept anything less than the passion, craziness, pleasure, pain, frustration, transparency and full disclosure that comes with true grown up love."
>
> –Grown up & Sexy

Grown up & Sexy – I chuckle at myself because I too only allow some access to the true woman that I am. I have put up a wall so many times, not wanting to give of myself for fear of being hurt all over again.

My mother suffered from mental illness and therefore my family lived with mental illness. When I first started dating, I thought I would be honest and share this information up front. After sharing my mother's history with the gentleman I was dating at the time, he replied, "I'm afraid that you will turn out like your mother." Now I had never heard these words until then, but the words and his abandonment crushed me. At that moment I thought, "Why didn't he look past the challenges I face and see me for who I am?" *"Why didn't he see the beauty in me?"*

"When I look in the mirror who do I see?"

> "I see a woman who did not allow someone else's fear to overtake me. I did not get knocked down, I am alive, I am content with who I am, and I am purposefully loving me."
>
> –Aubrey

Aubrey – many women who may have walked in your shoes can be empowered by your determination not to allow your circumstances become your reality.

Mirror, Mirror on the wall, who's the fairest of them all?

I made myself feel like a "fool", when no one else saw me as the "fool." My partners were diverse culturally, physically and intellectually. Their needs for my way to love them were very different from one another. **To answer the Mirror, Mirror question,** *I wanted to believe that I was of course the fairest of them all. The most significant relationships I have had in my life only experienced me in the context of what I was feeling within. In hindsight, I was incomplete and looked for affirmation and confirmation in ways that were destructive. They were unable to see the beauty in me as I was unable to see the beauty in myself. Because of my insecurities, I made allowances for empty promises, and a series of multiple disappointments. In turn, I made myself believe what they saw in me was a reflection of what the essence of my being was. I opened the space for them to define who I was in the context of their brokenness.*

When I look in the mirror who do I see?

I see a woman who has many layers. I see a woman who experienced commitment in various ways and multiple chambers. I began to normalize my non-committal ways and disconnect from the possibility of a deeper relationship and connection. What I thought was overlooked, was never really uncovered and exposed. My past experiences brought me to really ask the questions: how did I get here ... in this place of utter rejection, depletion, failure? That's when I realized I was being pruned. I had so much to unload, and so much to discover that the journey lasted nearly a decade. I lived in contradictions and did not have the tolerance for development needed for the relationships to work.

"I now approach my beauty and blessings very differently. I am working on building tolerance and patience to look at the things from a different perspective and try to understand. I am better at being clear at defining what I want and articulating the same with the one who chooses to go on the journey with me. I am a lifelong learner in life and love. I am open to the possibilities and building tolerance for the exploration of extra-ordinary experiences."

–BayB'O

BayB'O – I have lived a life of layers that over the years I continue to allow God to shed from the hurt and pain. Each layer I continue to cleanse myself from the rejection and failures. I'm learning to love who I see in the mirror.

After having this virtual discussion and hearing about these powerful women's stories of hope and determination on how they overcame finding the beauty that was within all of them, I realized our strength and determination are how we begin realizing our purpose. That purpose is to find the beauty that lies within you. We have to stop wailing in our pit. There's an inner beauty about a woman whose confidence comes from those teachable moments … all those which have just been shared. **Why Didn't He See the Beauty in Me? because I saw the beauty in myself!**

Resources

1. *Integrity: Doing the Right Thing for the Right Reason.* McGill-Queen's University Press. 2010. p. 12. *ISBN 9780773582804.* Retrieved 2013-10-15. Integrity is a personal choice, an uncompromising and predictably consistent commitment to honor moral, ethical, spiritual, and artistic values and principles.

2. *Debianddrrob.com*

3. *Liveluvcreate.com*

4. *www.AwesomeQuotes4U.com*

5. *Simplereminders.com*

6. *Favim.com*

7. *Baggagerclaim.co.uk*

8. *Factsaboutyou/tumble*

9. *Quozio.com*

10. *Brainyquote.com*

11. *Live Your Truth. www.dougdoeslife.com*

12. *www.butterflylane.com*

13. *Yourbeautifullife.org*

14. *Heartfeltquotes.BLOGSPOTS.com*

15 Willow tree facts. Soft Schools. *www.softschools.com/facts/plants/Willow_tree_facts/555*

16 Self-Validation/Psychology Today. *www.psychologytoday.com/blog/pieces-mind/201407/self-validation*

17 *She-Tribe.com*

18 *Abouteverythingblogspot.com*

19 *www.stevemaraboli.com*

20 *Purehappylife.com*

21 *Quotepixel.com*

22 AZ Quotes

23 Holy Bible; Proverbs 10:7, 1 Peter 3:3-4 NIV, Genesis 1:27 New American Standard, II Corinthians 5:7 NKJV, 1 Peter 5:5-7, Psalm 46:1, Hebrew 11:1 NKJV, Psalms 139:14 NKJV, Psalms 1:3, Genesis 37:5-36; 39, 20-23; 41:14-44, PROVERB 3:21-23 New Living Translation (NLT), Philippians 4:13 NKJV

24 Merriam-Webster Dictionary

About the Author

Verleaner R. Lane, MA. author and the Associate Director with University of Illinois at Urbana-Champaign, is a contracted employee with the Illinois Department of Children and Family Services, Office of Learning and Professional Development. Verleaner has over 28 years of child welfare experience, working with children and families.

Writing this book, she wanted to empower women and girls about their brokenness when they go around looking like they've got it all together. She wants to challenge who we really see in the mirror. She wanted to share her personal experiences dealing with divorce and some challenging relationships. This was a time of healing for all of the baggage she carried around from one relationship to another, even after she thought she cleaned the suitcase out but some small particle of him was left behind.

Verleaner is a dedicated member of St. John Missionary Baptist Church *"a church where everybody is somebody"*. Over the last eleven years Verleaner has been the Coordinator for the Dr. AED Youth Choir, Soprano Section Leader for the Mass Choir. She also works with the Christian Education Ministry where she trains the leaders of the church in various workshops.

She is a proud alumnus of Lane Technical High School. Verleaner completed her undergraduate work at Northern Illinois University where she obtained a Bachelor of Arts in Sociology/Criminology. Ms. Lane attended graduate studies at Governor State University with a Master of Art's in Early Childhood Education.

You can find Verleaner being a servant working hard in the vineyard with the Top Ladies of Distinction Will County Black Diamond Chapter, where she is one of the chartering members. She is one of the co-founders for Divas Down for The Cause, Inc. a charitable organization dedicated to supporting and empowering individuals; transforming their life challenges into opportunities for success. Verleaner Lane is a native of Chicago. She currently is single and lives in South Holland, IL.